Prezi Cookbook

Over 100 simple but incredible recipes to create dynamic, engaging, and beautiful presentations using Prezi

Charlotte Olsson

Christina Hoyer

PUBLISHING

BIRMINGHAM - MUMBAI

Prezi Cookbook

First published: April 2015

Production reference: 1310315

Published by Packt Publishing Ltd.
Livery Place
35 Livery Street
Birmingham B3 2PB, UK.

ISBN 978-1-78355-183-5

www.packtpub.com

Credits

About the Authors

Charlotte Olsson is a certified Prezi expert. She has studied adult pedagogy and psychology. She has worked with Prezi since 2011 and has over 12 years of experience as a software trainer.

In 2012, Charlotte cofounded Imprezzing, which specializes in Prezi solutions.

Charlotte is a gifted communicator. She loves Prezi because it helps companies and individuals share their stories. Since 2011, she has been providing Prezi training and Prezi designs to a wide range of companies worldwide. Her expertise and solutions are praised by all her clients.

Charlotte is based in California, where she manages Imprezzing's operations in the U.S.

Thank you everyone who urged me to believe and move forward. You guys made the difference, and I could not have written this book without you.

Christina Hoyer is a cofounding partner of Imprezzing and has worked with Prezi since 2010. She is the owner and manager of Imprezzing Scandinavia. Based in Copenhagen, she provides training, design, and complete Prezi implementations for companies and organizations throughout Scandinavia (in Danish and English).

Christina is a certified Prezi expert and is active within the international community of Prezi experts. She has a master's degree in arts and business management, and is experienced in strategic communication and presentations mentoring. Since 2004, she has been the CEO of her own company.

Christina is a sought-after keynote speaker and has authored a Danish book about presentation skills, named *Tag ordet I din magt - en værktøjskasse for talere.*

Thank you friends, colleagues, and family for the encouragement, input, and loving support in the wee hours.

About the Reviewers

Marthe Bijman is the president of Red Pennant Communications, a marketing communications and branding consultancy company that she founded in 2006. She is a writer, literature critic, and marketing communications specialist. Her particular areas of specialization are branding, social media, and change management communications. She has worked extensively in the mining and information technology industries. She holds a BA degree, a BA honors in literature, a BA honors in journalism, an H.Dip.Ed in language teaching, and an MA in applied linguistics and literary sciences. Marthe publishes book reviews and analyses on her literary blog at www.sevencircumstances.com. Her blog on business writing and marketing is available at www.red-pennant-communications.com. A reputed author and South African born, she now resides in Vancouver, Canada.

Tara Das is a government information librarian at Columbia University. She has a PhD in anthropology and political science and an MPH in quantitative methods.

Isidro Landa, Jr is currently a graduate student in a master's program in psychological research at California State University, Long Beach (CSULB). He received his BA in psychology with honors from CSULB in 2014. His involvement in research has helped him cultivate writing, critical thinking, and statistical skills.

Isidro has traveled to state and national conferences to present his work, some of which included Prezi presentations in formal research competitions. Through research, he seeks to better understand the psychosocial factors that influence positive socio-emotional development in adolescents and young adults, particularly in educational settings. Though he is fascinated by theoretical research, he is equally passionate about the applied aspects of his line of work.

Isidro practices Vipassana meditation and trains in Krav Maga in his free time.

Nida Siddiqui is a lecturer of mathematics at the University of Sharjah, UAE. She is an IBM Certified SPSS specialist and a laboratory supervisor at the mathematics department of the University of Sharjah. While her research interests are applied mathematics in general and differential equations in particular, she also works as an educationist by applying integrated technology in teaching design for undergraduate studies.

Nida holds a certified degree in education and has experience of teaching across British and American curriculums along with IB at the high school and university level.

Reviewing the Prezi Cookbook has been an educational experience. This book is very well-written and caters to the needs of individuals at all levels of study. I would like to thank Packt Publishing for entrusting me with this task, and my family for their continual support.

www.PacktPub.com

Support files, eBooks, discount offers, and more

For support files and downloads related to your book, please visit www.PacktPub.com.

Did you know that Packt offers eBook versions of every book published, with PDF and ePub files available? You can upgrade to the eBook version at www.PacktPub.com and as a print book customer, you are entitled to a discount on the eBook copy. Get in touch with us at service@packtpub.com for more details.

At www.PacktPub.com, you can also read a collection of free technical articles, sign up for a range of free newsletters and receive exclusive discounts and offers on Packt books and eBooks.

https://www2.packtpub.com/books/subscription/packtlib

Do you need instant solutions to your IT questions? PacktLib is Packt's online digital book library. Here, you can search, access, and read Packt's entire library of books.

Why subscribe?

- ► Fully searchable across every book published by Packt
- ► Copy and paste, print, and bookmark content
- ► On demand and accessible via a web browser

Free access for Packt account holders

If you have an account with Packt at www.PacktPub.com, you can use this to access PacktLib today and view 9 entirely free books. Simply use your login credentials for immediate access.

Table of Contents

Preface

Prezi is the presentation tool of the future. Its amazing canvas lets you easily create presentations that have high impact. Unlike traditional presentation software, Prezi allows you to create non-linear presentations that easily embed your own content or content from the web and can be easily shared via URL links.

It is easy to understand and enables you to create eye-catching presentations that can captivate and impress your audience. The secret? Prezi combines a non-slide format that gives you the freedom to combine text, images, and other materials in new and great ways. Add some of the zooms and turns that make Prezi stand out, and you will stand strong as a presenter.

With this book, you will learn how professionals build their presentations using Prezi quickly and efficiently. In short, in this book we make it easy and straightforward for you to work with Prezi.

What this book covers

Chapter 1, Administer Your Account and Your Prezi, teaches you how to create, save, and locate your prezis and also set their access through privacy settings. You will see how to arrange your prezis using a Prezi folder system. Renaming the folder and sharing it with your colleagues are some of the tasks that you can perform on the folders.

Chapter 2, Inserting Text, Images, and Links, teaches you how to work on the Prezi canvas, and how to work with text and images. You will learn to apply templates, and use different methods to insert and edit text and images.

Chapter 3, Symbols and Shapes, Lines and Arrows, deals with symbols and shapes, a useful collection of simple graphic items that you can easily insert on the canvas to enhance it. You will also learn about arrows and lines that are attractive and useful in your presentations.

Chapter 4, Editing Elements on the Canvas, teaches you how to work with texts, images, videos, frames, and other such elements on your canvas. You will learn how to resize, turn, move, group, and layer these elements.

Chapter 5, Path and Steps, shows how to arrange the elements on your canvas and show them in a specific order. Elements that can be used as steps are anything that you can put on the canvas; texts, image, videos, symbols, shapes, grouped elements, PDF, and so on. You will learn to create steps, and how to create and edit a path in Prezi.

Chapter 6, Frames and Prezi Ratio, will cover frames, which are an integral part of how Prezi works. You will learn to add and remove content in frames, group and organize them, and control how the content is presented. This chapter also shows how to set the overall ratio for your prezi, and how this setting reflects on your frames so that they automatically match the required screen proportions.

Chapter 7, Zoom and Turn, provides a hands-on approach to learning zooms and turns. When zooms and turns are used correctly, they become powerful tools that greatly enhance your prezi. You will see how to create them, how to combine them with each other, and how they can be applied to all the elements we insert on the canvas.

Chapter 8, Animation, teaches you how to make animations. It shows how to create them and how to edit and reset your animations. It will also show you how to fade a group of elements.

Chapter 9, Reuse Favorite Frames and Elements, will go in-depth into Prezi's advanced features. Knowing how to transfer and reuse a number of elements or whole sections between the prezis in your Prezi account enables you to reuse material, so that you will not have to spend time recreating what you already created once.

Chapter 10, Media Files in Prezi, will be a fun chapter to read because media enhances your presentations in great ways and is so easy to add to your prezi. Adding speech and background music to your prezi or adding videos will be great enhancements.

Chapter 11, Templates, Colors, and Fonts, will teach you how to choose, use, and edit Prezi templates. Using Theme Wizard, you can customize the look of your prezi.

Chapter 12, Presenting with Prezi, covers all the functions in Prezi's present mode. With this chapter, Prezi's presenting features become easy to learn and understand, making it possible for all presenters to feel at home with these functions.

Chapter 13, Prezi on Other Devices, will show you how to work with Prezi for Windows/Mac and Prezi for iPhone/iPad. You will also learn how to create your prezis offline using the Prezi App.

Chapter 14, PowerPoint and Prezi, will explore three different methods for importing material from a PowerPoint presentation onto your Prezi canvas.

Chapter 15, _Sharing and Collaborating_, shows how to collaborate real time in Prezi to allow your colleagues to do real-time editing on your prezis and also shows you how to give your presentations in collaborative mode. Using the portable feature of Prezi, you can download and show your prezi anywhere.

Appendix A, _Design_, explores the basic design principles that will actively support and strengthen your prezi.

Appendix B, _Transitions_, covers how you can make your presentation move forward smoothly in the present mode.

Appendix C, _Keyboard Shortcuts_, has a collection of shortcuts that can be used during presentation and for editing your prezis.

What you need for this book

To work online in Prezi, use your computer and your Internet connection.

A downloadable version of Prezi is offered to paying subscribers. This allows you to work in Prezi without being online.

Prezi offers free apps that allow all Prezi users to access the program and their presentations using their smartphone and iPad.

Who this book is for

This book is for everyone who is interested in using Prezi for personal or professional use. This book has a series of thorough and easy-to-read recipes. You may read it from start to end for complete Prezi education, or use it as a reference guide for specific questions.

We want you to start using Prezi NOW. Don't spend hours and hours studying. With this book, you can work in Prezi right away.

Sections

In this book, you will find several headings that appear frequently (Getting ready, How to do it, How it works, There's more, and See also).

To give clear instructions on how to complete a recipe, we use these sections as follows:

Getting ready

This section tells you what to expect in the recipe, and describes how to set up any software or any preliminary settings required for the recipe.

How to do it...

This section contains the steps required to follow the recipe.

How it works...

This section usually consists of a detailed explanation of what happened in the previous section.

There's more...

This section consists of additional information about the recipe in order to make the reader more knowledgeable about the recipe.

See also

This section provides helpful links to other useful information for the recipe.

Conventions

In this book, you will find a number of styles of text that distinguish between different kinds of information. Here are some examples of these styles, and an explanation of their meaning.

Words that you see on the screen, in menus or dialog boxes for example, appear in the text like this: "The **Enjoy** account is a subscription that you pay for, after the first month".

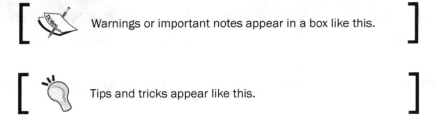

Warnings or important notes appear in a box like this.

Tips and tricks appear like this.

Reader feedback

Feedback from our readers is always welcome. Let us know what you think about this book—what you liked or may have disliked. Reader feedback is important for us to develop titles that you really get the most out of.

To send us general feedback, simply send an e-mail to feedback@packtpub.com, and mention the book title via the subject of your message.

If there is a topic that you have expertise in and you are interested in either writing or contributing to a book, see our author guide on www.packtpub.com/authors.

Customer support

Now that you are the proud owner of a Packt book, we have a number of things to help you to get the most from your purchase.

Downloading the color images of this book

We also provide you a PDF file that has color images of the screenshots/diagrams used in this book. The color images will help you better understand the changes in the output. You can download this file from: http://www.packtpub.com/sites/default/files/downloads/prezicookbook_colorimages.pdf.

Errata

Although we have taken every care to ensure the accuracy of our content, mistakes do happen. If you find a mistake in one of our books—maybe a mistake in the text or the code—we would be grateful if you would report this to us. By doing so, you can save other readers from frustration and help us improve subsequent versions of this book. If you find any errata, please report them by visiting http://www.packtpub.com/submit-errata, selecting your book, clicking on the **errata submission form** link, and entering the details of your errata. Once your errata are verified, your submission will be accepted and the errata will be uploaded on our website, or added to any list of existing errata, under the Errata section of that title. Any existing errata can be viewed by selecting your title from http://www.packtpub.com/support.

Piracy

Piracy of copyright material on the Internet is an ongoing problem across all media. At Packt, we take the protection of our copyright and licenses very seriously. If you come across any illegal copies of our works, in any form, on the Internet, please provide us with the location address or website name immediately so that we can pursue a remedy.

Please contact us at copyright@packtpub.com with a link to the suspected pirated material.

We appreciate your help in protecting our authors, and our ability to bring you valuable content.

Questions

You can contact us at questions@packtpub.com if you are having a problem with any aspect of the book, and we will do our best to address it.

1
Administer Your Account and Your Prezi

In this chapter, we will cover the following recipes:

- ▶ Choosing the right Prezi account
- ▶ The account overview window (your prezi)
- ▶ Creating a new prezi
- ▶ Saving your prezi
- ▶ Finding an existing prezi
- ▶ Creating a folder
- ▶ Renaming a folder
- ▶ Showing the prezi of a specific folder
- ▶ Removing a prezi from a folder
- ▶ Sharing a folder
- ▶ Deleting a folder
- ▶ Privacy settings

Introduction

This chapter describes the various Prezi accounts, and helps you choose among them.

After setting up your account, you will want to start working in Prezi. To do this, you need to know how to create, save, and locate your prezis.

As you create more prezis, you will need to organize them using Prezi's folder system.

Finally, depending on your account type, you may want to adjust the privacy settings for one or more of your prezis.

In this chapter, you will find recipes that take you by the hand and make it easy to perform all of these actions.

Choosing the right Prezi account

Prezi offers different accounts for different users. In the following screenshot, you will find a description of them all, starting with the simplest setup:

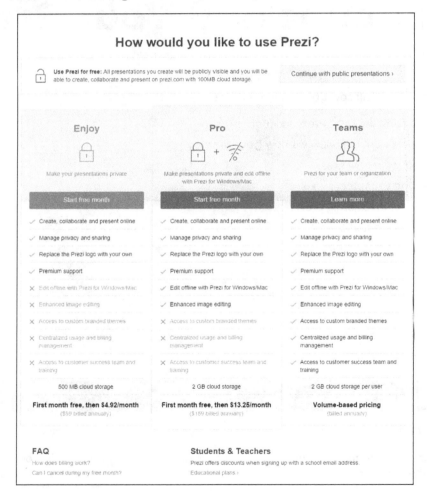

You will find this Prezi account overview at `www.Prezi.com/pricing`.

The Continue with public presentations account

The public account is 100 percent free. With it, you have full online access to the Prezi program except for a few picture editing tools. Your prezis will be public, meaning that anyone can view them on the Internet. You will have 100 MB storage for your prezis, which is fine for most start up users.

The Enjoy account

The **Enjoy** account is a subscription that you pay for after the first month. One of the great features that apply to the paid accounts is the privacy option. This option allows you to choose with whom (if anyone) you want to share your prezis. It also allows you to insert your own logo into your presentations, and gives you better support and 500 MB storage. The **Enjoy** account offers limited access to some of Prezi's picture editing tools.

The Pro account

The **Pro** account is a subscription that you pay for. The huge benefit of the **Pro** account is that you can download the Prezi program to your computer (Windows or Mac). Use this account to work in Prezi without being online. With this account comes 2 GB online storage for your presentations, and you will have access to all of Prezi's picture editing tools.

The Teams account

The **Teams** account is used for businesses and offers the option of storing custom Prezi templates called "branded themes" and centralized billing, which makes it easy to administer several accounts. You are also offered easier access to support and 500 MB storage.

The Edu account

Students and teachers are offered educational accounts. The educational accounts are called **Edu Enjoy**, **Edu Pro**, and **Edu Teams**. These accounts are the same as the accounts described beforehand, but are offered to students and teachers at a reduced price. You are eligible for an educational plan if you sign up for your edu-Prezi account using a school e-mail address.

The account overview window (your prezis)

Logging into your Prezi account takes you to your account overview window.

How to use it...

The account overview shows a list of all your prezis and all your folders (when created), as shown in the following screenshot:

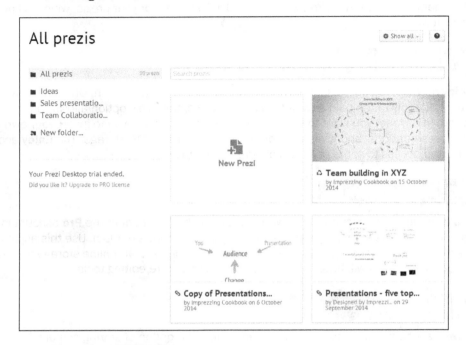

Why do you need it?

Use the account overview to:

▶ Access any of your existing prezis

▶ Create and administrate your folders

▶ Create a new prezi

There's more...

When working in a prezi, you can access the account overview window for all your prezis at any time by clicking on the **Your prezis** tab in the browser window.

Creating a new prezi

Open your browser and go to www.Prezi.com. Log in to your Prezi account.

To create a new prezi, click on the **New Prezi** icon in the account overview window, as shown in the following screenshot:

Clicking on **New Prezi** opens a new browser tab where you will create your new prezi.

 This is the only way to create a new prezi. You cannot open a new prezi from within an existing presentation, nor are there keys you can use to do it. Kind of nice and simple!

Saving your Prezi

There are three ways to save a prezi after working on the canvas:

- Click on *Ctrl + S*
- Use the **Save** icon
- Exit the prezi

Saving with the save icon

While working in Prezi, you can click on the **Save** icon to save at any time. The icon is placed over the canvas to the left, as shown in the following screenshot:

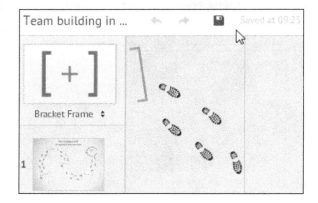

This is a saving feature that also runs automatically. Whenever you apply a change to your prezi, this change is autosaved. It is not possible to disable autosave.

 If you want to experiment with the content in an existing prezi, create a copy of it to do your experimenting here. This way autosaved changes will not affect your existing work.

Saving with close and exit

A prezi is also automatically saved whenever you exit the prezi using the **Exit** button in the upper-right corner of the Prezi screen. Exit (and save) a prezi by clicking on the **Exit** button in the upper-right corner of the Prezi window.

A prezi is always saved when you click on the **Exit** button.

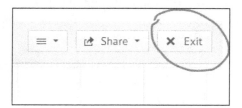

Finding an existing prezi

Clicking on **Your prezis** opens the account overview window for your prezi files. All your prezis are listed here as thumbnails.

From here, you can either go directly into editing mode or you can access file handling features for a prezi.

How to do it...

Hovering over a prezi's thumbnail gives you access to the icons that you can use to edit or share your prezi. Hovering over a thumbnail produces the **Edit**, **Share**, **Folder**, and **Delete** icons. The trash icon to the right can be used to delete the prezi as shown in the following screenshot:

To access the full range of file handling features for a prezi, begin by clicking on its thumbnail in the account overview window. This opens the prezi-handling window for that prezi. Here you see your prezi in a small window, as shown in the following screenshot:

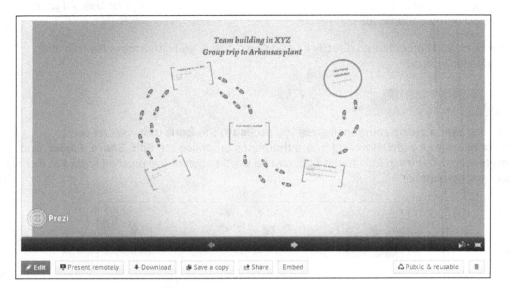

At the bottom of the prezi-handling window, you'll find forward and backward arrows that you can click to navigate through the prezi. For faster navigation, use the blue slider tool (visible after hovering over the black navigation bar at the bottom of the window).

Below the prezi-handling window is a toolbar with various options to handle your prezi. The options are as follows:

- Use **Edit** to access editing mode for your prezi
- Use **Present remotely** to start a remote presentation (please refer to *Chapter 12, Presenting with Prezi*, to learn about presenting)
- Use the **Download** button to download your prezi (please refer to *Chapter 15, Sharing and Collaborating*, to learn more about the download of prezis)
- Use the **Save a copy** option to create a copy of your Prezi (this copy will be immediately accessible in your account overview window)
- The **Share** option allows you to share a prezi in different ways (please refer to *Chapter 15, Sharing and Collaborating*, to learn about sharing)
- Use the **Embed** button to create a small piece of code to use for embedding the prezi on your website (please refer to *Chapter 15, Sharing and Collaborating*, to learn more about embedding)

The **Public & reusable** button shows the current privacy choice for your prezi. (Please refer to the *Privacy settings* section of this chapter to read more about this.)

The trash icon to the very right can be used to delete this prezi.

Creating a folder

Folders in Prezi allow you to organize your prezi in categories. Once your prezi are assigned to folders, you can access a specific selection (the prezi in a folder) of your prezi so that you will not have to go through your complete portfolio to find a specific prezi.

 Click on the **All Prezis** folder to see all your prezis in the account overview window.

Getting ready

The Prezi folders are accessed via the account overview window. On the left side of this window, you will find two folder icons named **All Prezis** and **New folder**. Click on **All Prezis** to see prezis from all folders.

 The account overview is shown when you access your Prezi account. If you are already working in a prezi, you can always click the browser tab on **Your prezis** to go to your account overview window.

How to do it...

Perform the following steps to create a new folder:

1. Click on **New folder** to create a new folder. This opens the name box.

2. Assign a relevant name to the folder by writing a name in the box provided. The maximum length for a name is 17 characters.

3. To save it, click on **Rename**.

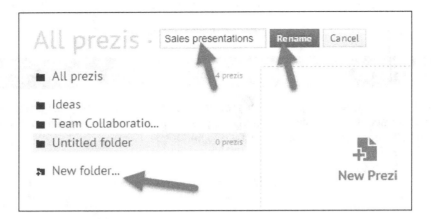

 Create as many folders as you like. Do it now or later.

Renaming a folder

Sometimes, names for your folders don't fit so well any more, and you want to change them. Fortunately, this is easily done.

How to do it...

Perform the following steps to rename a folder:

1. Click on the folder in the folder list on the left.
2. Write a new name in the name box (highlighted).
3. Click on **Rename** to save the name.

Take a look at the following screenshot:

Getting ready

To add a prezi to a folder, access the account overview window. Locate the thumbnail for the prezi that you want to assign to a folder.

How to do it...

1. Hover over the thumbnail. This produces a row of prezi-handling icons at the top of the thumbnail.

2. Locate the folder icon. Click on it to open the drop-down menu that lists all the folders you previously created, as shown in the following screenshot:

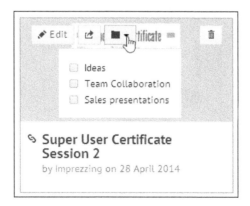

3. Check one or more of the boxes in the drop-down menu to choose which folder(s) you want to assign the prezi to.

 A prezi can be assigned to one or multiple folders.

Showing the prezi of a specific folder

To view the prezis that have been assigned to a specific folder, click on that folder in the folder list, as shown in the following screenshot:

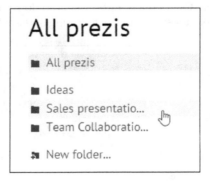

 Adding a prezi to a folder does not create a copy of this prezi. Consequently, if a folder holds a prezi that you think does not belong in that folder, do not delete the prezi. Instead, hover over the thumbnail to show the icons, click on the **Folder** icon and deselect the checkbox next to any folder you do not want the prezi assigned to.

Removing a Prezi from a folder

Whether you are reorganizing your system of folders and need to move a lot of prezis around or you just decide to remove a single prezi from a folder, it is easy to do.

How to do it...

1. To remove a prezi from a folder, go to the account overview window.
2. Hover over the prezi's thumbnail to show the prezi-handling icons.
3. Click on the **Folder** icon.
4. Unassign a prezi from a folder by removing the checkmark for this folder, as shown in the following screenshot:

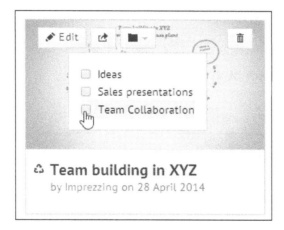

Sharing a folder

Sharing folders is an easy way to allow others to view your presentations. Sharing a folder with a friend or a colleague means that you allow that person to view the prezis in that specific folder.

How to do it...

1. Click on the folder that you want to share.

2. Click on the **Add viewer** tab above your thumbnails, or click on the cogwheel right next to it. Both options are shown in the following screenshot:

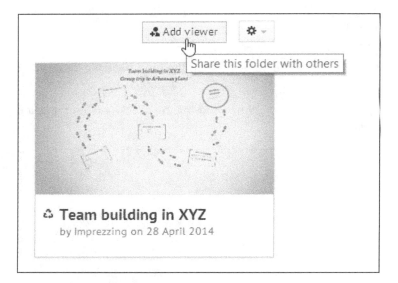

There's more...

The person sharing your folder will not be able to edit your prezi.

 You can share prezis and folders with people whose e-mails are associated to a specific Prezi account.

See also

▶ Please refer to *Chapter 15, Sharing and Collaborating*, to learn about sharing and/or allowing editing rights to another Prezi account holder.

Deleting a folder

If a folder becomes obsolete, it is easy to remove.

How to do it...

1. Go to the account overview window.

2. Click to select the folder that you want to delete.

3. Click on the cogwheel to the right of your prezi thumbnail. Deleting a folder does not delete the prezis assigned to it. Take a look at the following screenshot:

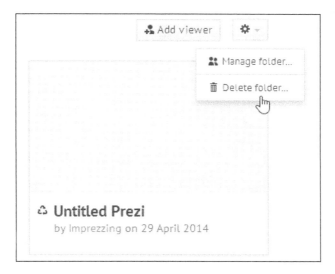

There's more...

Deleting a folder does not delete the prezis in it. This is because folders do not store copies of your prezis. Folders are only a means to view a selection of prezis.

Privacy settings

If you are using a free account, your prezis will always be public. Users of **Enjoy**, **Pro**, **Team**, and **Edu** accounts have several options for the privacy settings of a prezi. The other options are **Hidden** (the prezi can be seen by you and those who have a link) and **Private** (only you can view the prezi).

How to do it...

1. Access the account overview window.

2. Click on the thumbnail for the prezi whose privacy settings you want to adjust.

3. Click on **Public** to the right beneath the prezi window.

4. The privacy window is now open. Adjust the privacy for a prezi by choosing from **Private**, **Hidden**, and **Public**. Take a look at the following screenshot:

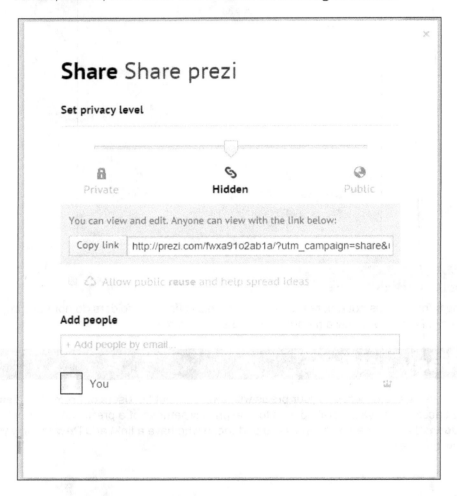

Now choose either **Private**, **Hidden**, **Public**, or **Reusable**.

There's more...

If you think that other people might benefit from using your prezi, why not allow them to do so? All it takes is a few clicks of your mouse.

Make the prezi public by dragging the privacy slider all the way to the right. Then put a check mark in the box next to **Allow public reuse and help spread ideas**.

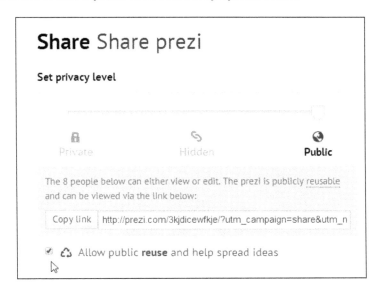

Click on the **Explore** tab above your account overview window to view and access all reusable prezis on Prezi's site.

2

Inserting Text, Images, and Links

In this chapter, we will cover the following recipes:

- ▶ Choosing a Prezi template
- ▶ Navigating the Prezi canvas
- ▶ Working with text in Prezi
- ▶ Multiple textboxes for different styles
- ▶ Copying and pasting text and images
- ▶ Inserting images from your computer
- ▶ Inserting images from Google/Flickr
- ▶ Editing the images by cropping
- ▶ Using effects of Prezi's photo editor
- ▶ Understanding image file types in Prezi
- ▶ Inserting hyperlinks

Introduction

This chapter covers how to work on the Prezi canvas, and how to work with text and images. You will learn to apply templates and use different methods to insert and edit text and images.

Before we begin teaching you all the good stuff, it is important that you know that Prezi's editing tools are organized in two structures with some overlap of commands. We have the right-click menu, and we have the black toolbar that appears over a selected item, as shown in the following screenshot:

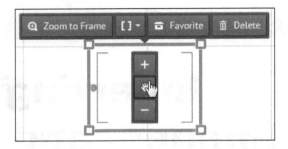

When you activate these tools, their options will be different depending on the item that you are working with. As an example, you will have different options to edit a frame versus text.

Some of the tools are only available in the right-click menu (such as rearranging your layers), so be sure to check out both tools when you are editing an item.

Choosing a Prezi template

Getting ready

When you create a new prezi, the first step is always choosing a template. There is no way to create a prezi without the use of a template.

Prezi offers a wide range of templates with graphics and frames. If you wish to design your prezi from scratch (without any imagery, and only a minimum of frames and placeholders for text), choose the template called "Blank".

How to do it...

1. Click on the **New Prezi** icon in the account overview window.
2. Use the **Choose your template** window to view the many designs.
3. Click on **More** to view the complete collection.
4. Click on the template you want to use.
5. Click on **Use template** to create the prezi.

There is a shortcut to create a blank prezi, the white button to the left of **Use template**, as shown in the following screenshot:

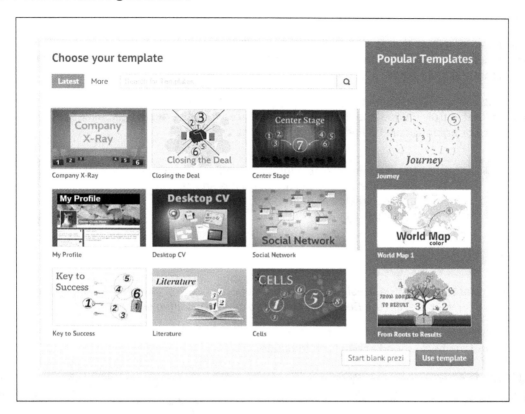

How it works...

The ready-made templates offer a huge variety, not only in looks, but in structure and content as well. This is because the different templates serve different purposes. Some templates are structured to describe a process, others to support a message about a conflict, and others will be great to illustrate a forward-moving storyline.

The templates offer a variety of color schemes. For some of the templates, you can edit the underlying graphics and the color scheme, for others you cannot. To best support your message, choose colors that will appeal to your audience and match your subject.

In Prezi, the visuals are an integrated part of your message. When you choose a template or edit your design, it is very important that the visuals reflect your message in style and structure.

There's more...

Be aware that using the pre-designed templates in Prezi presents a potential pitfall.

Using the templates that Prezi supplies means using a template that others use too. This creates a risk for identical presentations at a meeting or for someone in your audience having seen that template before.

Starting your prezi based on the blank template (called **Blank**) gives you the option to create a prezi that is truly unique and that can be customized to fit the design guidelines for your company or organization 100 percent.

 Use the templates to educate yourself on prezi design. Study the color schemes and the use of frames and path in these templates that are created by professional designers. Reuse all the ideas that you like in your own prezis.

See also

Please refer to *Appendix A, Design*, to read more about choosing the right template and structure for your prezi in the *Basic design principles–composition* section.

Please refer to *Chapter 11, Templates, Colors, and Fonts*, to learn about changing colors, fonts, and the background image for a template.

Navigating through the Prezi canvas

The canvas in Prezi is our working area. This is where we insert or create every item that we want to have in our prezi.

The canvas is flexible in many ways. It is a three-dimensional canvas, which means that we can work not only on the horizontal and vertical planes, but also in depth, by zooming in and out.

Prezi users often ask us "How big is the canvas?" or "How much can you zoom in Prezi?". These questions are very relevant and we are happy to answer because it is all good news: the canvas is potentially huge, and you can zoom a lot.

There are no set numbers or measurements to describe the exact size or depth of the Prezi canvas. When you reach Prezi's limits for width or depth of the canvas, you will get a message saying something like "**Cannot zoom in/out more**" or "**Cannot pan more**". These limits cannot be changed and you must adjust your content to fit the limits for the canvas area and depths.

However, the canvas is huge in width and depth and you will only seldom experience that you cannot move in a direction or depth.

The canvas in Prezi is large, flexible, and three-dimensional. Before you begin creating prezis, we recommend that you spend a few minutes to familiarize yourself with how the canvas works.

Getting ready

Create a new prezi by clicking on the **New Prezi** icon in the account overview window. Your new prezi opens in edit mode. Edit mode is where you see the Prezi canvas and the controls that you will use to create your content and edit the prezi. The following screenshot shows prezi in edit mode:

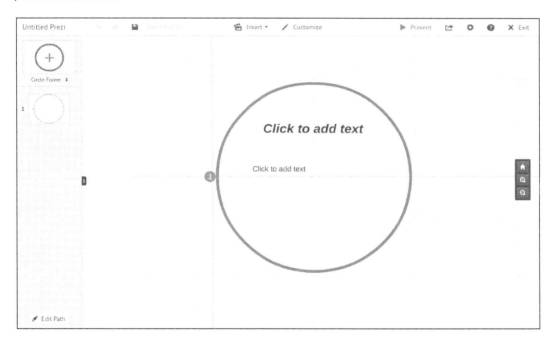

An overview of the canvas

On the canvas is a small toolbar that allows you to get an overview of your canvas. It is placed to the very right, midway vertically. The toolbar becomes visible when you hover your mouse over this area. It has three options, which are as follows:

▸ **House/Home**: This option adjusts your canvas to show a complete overview of all items on your Prezi canvas

▸ **Magnifying glass +**: This option zooms into the canvas

> ▸ **Magnifying glass -**: This option zooms out of the canvas

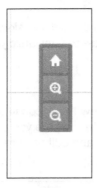

 If you ever feel that you've gotten lost on your canvas and don't know what's up and down or where you currently are, click on the House/Home icon to zoom in/out to a complete overview of your canvas.

How to do it...

Because the canvas is large, we sometimes need to move it around (to the sides or up and down) to access areas that are currently not visible on our computer screen. Moving the canvas is easy! Just use your mouse to:

1. Click anywhere on the canvas

2. Hold the left mouse key down

3. Move the canvas by dragging to the sides or up and down

Zoom on the canvas

The Prezi canvas has depth and you can insert and access content on any zoom level. It is easy to do! Using the scroll wheel on your mouse is the easiest way to zoom in and out. Notice where your mouse is pointing as you turn the wheel. This position on the canvas is where you are zooming into or out from.

 Clicking and holding an element towards the visible edge of the canvas will move (push) the canvas to allow room for that element.

Familiarize yourself with zooming techniques in *Chapter 7, Zoom and Turn*.

Working with text in Prezi

Working with text in Prezi is very easy. All work with text is done in textboxes.

How to do it...

1. Click (once) anywhere on the canvas to create an open textbox.
2. Type in the textbox or paste copied text from another source into the box.
3. Click outside the textbox to close it.
4. To edit the text, reopen the textbox by clicking on it twice.

Take a look at the following screenshot:

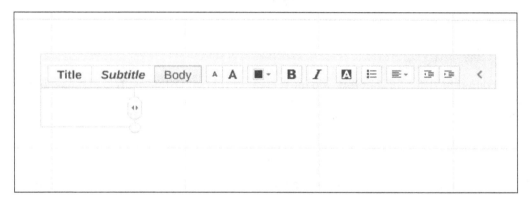

 If you don't want the new textbox you opened, cancel it by using the *Esc* key on your keyboard.

Textbox – an editing tool

The textbox shown in the previous screenshot is the toolbar that you will use for all text edits, except adjustments of size and turning.

To edit a previously created text, double-click on the text to access the textbox tools.

An open textbox offers a wide range of editing options. If a specific portion of text is selected, only this portion will be affected by the edits. Changes (edits) are applied to all the content in the textbox if you do not select a specific portion before applying.

Style options in the textbox

A style is a collection of settings for text. In Prezi, we can work with a maximum of three different styles for the text. These styles are Title, Subtitle, and Body.

A textbox can only have one kind of style in it, so any style that is chosen will affect all text in the textbox.

Click one of the three Prezi styles to apply it to your text. The following screenshot shows three different styles applied to the text in three textboxes:

There's more...

To use different styles for your text, you must create separate textboxes. This means that if you want to use the heading style and the body style, you create two separate textboxes. Read more about this in the *Multiple sections for different styles* section.

Other options in the textbox

Clicking on the icons circled in the following screenshot will change the text size in increments:

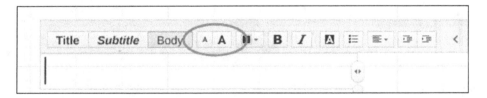

To change the fonts for the styles, please refer to *Chapter 11, Templates, Colors, and Fonts,* to understand how to do it and refer to *Appendix A, Design,* for suggestions on how to choose fonts for different purposes.

The following screenshot shows the black icon used to access the color palette:

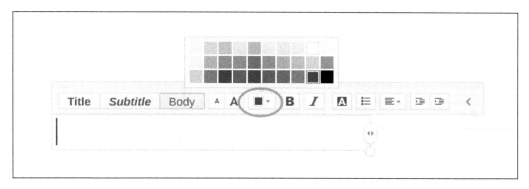

Clicking on the black icon opens the palette that allows you to change the color of the text. Select a portion of text to apply a color to that portion only, or just click on a color to apply to all text in the textbox. Then select a color by clicking on the palette.

Read more about applying colors in *Chapter 11, Templates, Colors, and Fonts*. Read more about colors as an element in your design in *Appendix A, Design*.

The following screenshot shows icons that can be used to apply bold or italics to your text:

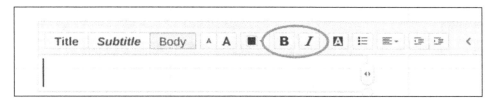

Use these icons to apply bold or italic style to your text. Click again to remove bold or italic and go back to regular style.

Select a portion of text to apply a bold or italic style to that portion only. If applied with no text selected, bold or italic style will be applied to all the text in the textbox.

The following screenshot shows an icon to apply the background color to your textbox:

Click on the icon shown in the previous screenshot to apply background color to the textbox. Background color will be applied to all content in the textbox.

The icon shown in the following screenshot is used to apply bullets to the text in the textbox:

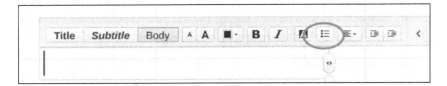

Click on the icon shown in the previous screenshot to apply bullets to your text. Bullets will be applied to the line you are currently working in, or all the text that you selected.

The icon shown in the following screenshot is used to choose the alignment for your text:

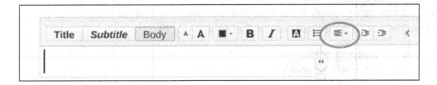

Click on the icon shown in the previous screenshot to choose the alignment for your text. The chosen alignment will be applied to the line you are currently working on, or all the text that you selected.

The icon shown in the following screenshot is used to apply indentation to the text:

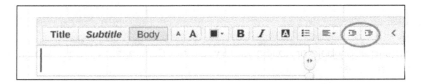

Click on the icon shown in the previous screenshot to apply indentation to your text. Indentation will be applied to the line that you are currently working in, or all the text that you selected.

The handle shown in the following screenshot is used to adjust the width of your textbox:

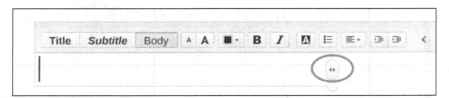

Dragging the handle with the double-headed arrow allows you to adjust the width of your textbox. You can make it very narrow, very wide, or anything in between, according to your taste and needs.

Dragging the circle corner of the handle will change or adjust the size of the text. The textbox will adjust to fit the size of the text in it. Take a look at the handle shown in the following screenshot:

There's more...

Most times, we adjust the size of the text without even opening the textbox. We have two different methods to do this.

Take a look at the following screenshot:

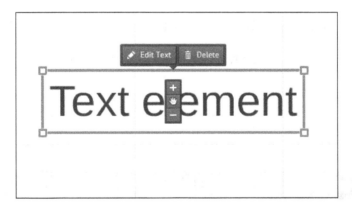

Click to select the text. The black toolbar opens. We have two options to adjust the size of the text:

- ▸ You can use the **+** and **–** signs to change the size in increments
- ▸ Alternatively, just click and hold one of the four square markers in the corners to pull or drag to resize the text

Multiple textboxes for different styles

The choice of font and size for a textbox applies to all the text in a box. This means that you will have to create individual textboxes for size and/or font variations in text design.

If you have already created the text and then realize that you want to add a different design to different parts of it, all you have to do is split the textbox into more textboxes. It is very easy to do.

How to do it...

1. Place the cursor in the line of text that you want to remove from the textbox.
2. Each separate text paragraph (one for each time you hit *Enter*) in a textbox has a handle. Place the cursor on a paragraph to see its handle.
3. Grab the handle to drag this paragraph out of the textbox.
4. Drop it anywhere on the canvas.

Take a look at the following screenshot:

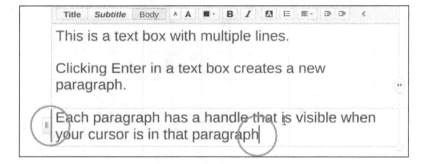

Copy and paste text and images

In Prezi, we use copying a lot because this is often the easiest and fastest way to create a copy that has the exact same size and settings as the original. We use it to copy all kinds of material such as text, images, videos, links, and frames.

Because Prezi is so flexible with size and angling of items, it can be hard or time-consuming to try and recreate a second item with the exact same settings as the original. On many occasions, it is often a good idea to copy and adjust an item instead of building it from scratch.

Prezi offers two methods of copying: duplicating, and copy and paste. They are both very easy and straightforward. Both methods can be used whether you want to copy just a single item or many items at a time. (You may want to read *Chapter 4, Editing Elements on the Canvas,* to learn about selecting multiple items.)

What is especially cool is that you can even use the copy and paste method to copy material from one prezi to another in your account.

Getting ready

Duplicating is a quick way to reuse material that you have in your prezi. It will help you save time by helping you avoid recreating or reimporting material that you already have in a prezi.

Open a prezi that has some kind of content on the canvas. We used an image file but any item will work.

How to do it...

Perform the following steps to duplicate an item:

1. Click on the item that you wish to duplicate, to select it.
2. Use the command *Ctrl + D* to create a duplicate item.

Perform the following steps to copy and paste an item:

1. Click on the item that you wish to copy, to select it.
2. Use *Ctrl + C* to copy the item to your clipboard.
3. Use *Ctrl + V* to insert the item on the Prezi canvas.

There's more...

The copy and paste method can also be used to copy items from one of your prezis to another. The feature will not work across different prezi accounts, but you can copy from one prezi to another that you have in one specific account.

The copy and paste method can even be used to copy text from a word processing program into Prezi. In these cases, any formatting does not get transferred, but you will get the full (unformatted) text inserted onto your canvas.

Inserting images from your computer

Images can be inserted onto the Prezi canvas from your computer, or from the Internet. In both cases, you will begin by going to the **Insert** menu and choosing **Image**.

How to do it...

One way to insert images into the Prezi canvas is as follows:

1. Go to the **Insert** menu.
2. Choose **Image**.
3. Use the dialogue box now available to the right of the Prezi canvas.
4. Click on **Select files** to access your computer.
5. Locate the image you want.
6. Insert it by selecting it and clicking on **Open** or by double-clicking the image, as shown in the following screenshot:

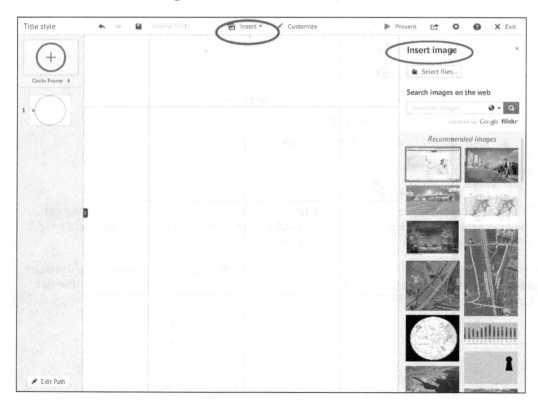

Another method is drag and drop. It is so easy to insert images in a prezi using this cool drag-it method. You don't even have to use the **Insert** menu to insert great images in your canvas. Perform the following steps to insert the images:

1. Share your screen between your prezi and your image folder. To do this, click on **Restore Down** (upper-right corner of the screen) for the prezi's window and the image folder's window to allow the open windows to fit side by side on your screen.

2. Locate the image that you want in your prezi.

3. Drag the image from the folder to the canvas (this will create a copy of your image), as shown in the following screenshot:

Pressing on the key *L* (use lower case) on your keyboard opens your filesystem for easy access to insert an image on the canvas.

See more shortcuts in *Appendix C*.

There's more...

Too many large images in your prezi can make your prezi's movements slow, and may cause it to not run smoothly during your presentation.

The maximum size for an image for Prezi is 2880 x 2880 pixels. You can safely insert at least 20 images as big as this in your prezi. If you insert more, it may cause the presentation to run less smoothly when presenting; worst case scenario being that it crashes and cannot run.

The solution is to only use large images when you need to zoom into them. And this is where Prezi actively lends a hand to help you.

When you are inserting a large image in your prezi, Prezi opens the dialog box as shown in the following screenshot to ask if you need the image to keep its current (large) size or if you prefer that Prezi resizes the image in order to make it smaller. Consider this as an offer! If you do not need to zoom into this image, click on **Resize image**. If you need the image to be large enough for close zooming, click on **Keep original**.

Inserting images from Google/Flickr

Let's now learn how to insert images from Google images and Flickr.

How to do it...

1. Go to the **Insert** menu.
2. Choose **Image**.
3. Use the dialog box now available to the right of the Prezi canvas.
4. Click on the search box just below the **Search images on the web** text.
5. Fill in a search term (such as climbing mountains, parrot, or whatever you need).
6. Click on the blue magnifying glass to start the search.
7. View the found images below the search box.

To insert one of these images on the canvas, just select, click, and drag the image from the sidebar to the canvas area. Take a look at the following screenshot:

Images for commercial use

If you are creating a prezi to use it for work or other professional purposes, you need to make sure that you are legally okay to show the images that you have in your prezi. When you buy images, you'll need to buy the right kind of license. When you are using Prezi's **Insert** function, you can filter your search to exclude images that are not licensed for commercial use:

1. Click on the triangle in the search field.
2. Go to the bottom of the small drop-down menu.
3. Put a checkmark next to **Show only images licensed for commercial use**.

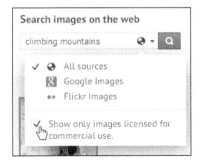

The authors of this book cannot guarantee that all images found through a filtered search as described are licensed for your commercial use.

Editing images by cropping

Prezi is a presentation tool. It is not designed to be your main source for image editing. However, it does provide a feature that allows you to crop your images. Check it out—it's fun.

How to do it...

Some images are beautiful but may contain an area that you do not need to show. In this case, you can use the cropping feature. (Cropping works like virtual scissors that let you "cut off" a slice of your image.) Perform the following steps to crop an image:

1. Click once on an image on your canvas to activate the toolbar for the image.
2. Choose **Crop Image**.
3. Pull the corner markers to control which portion of the image you want to show/hide.
4. Close the cropping tool by clicking outside the image (on the canvas) or by hitting *Esc* on your keyboard.

The original image is still present in your prezi. To change or reverse the cropping, just click on **Crop Image** again and reposition the markers.

Using effects of Prezi's photo editor

For subscribers to the **Pro** and **Edu Pro** accounts, Prezi offers a tool that lets you apply a number of different effects to your image. The tool is called photo editor. Despite its name, the photo editor works for all images (not just photos) provided the file type is `jpg`, `png`, or `gif`.

Open the **Photo Editor** by clicking on **Effects** on the toolbar above a selected image, as shown in the following screenshot:

How to do it...

1. Open the **Photo Editor** by clicking on the image that you want to edit.
2. Choose **Effects** on the toolbar to open the **Photo Editor**.
3. Click to choose the effect that you want to apply to your image.
4. Click on **Apply** to add an effect.
5. When you are done, click on **Save** to save your edits.

The photo editor offers a whole range of great effects that you can use to change your image. The options offered in the editor include great features, such as enhancing image color, changing the light, adding contrast, removing red eyes in portraits, and much more.

There's more...

Note that the photo editor offers a selection of frames that you can add to any image. Adding identical frames to images are a great way to create a more uniform look for the images in your prezi, even if they are quite different.

 Once you save an image with the applied effects, it is not reversible. Help yourself by duplicating your image before editing it (Click to select the image and press *Ctrl + D*).

Understanding image file types in Prezi

There is no set maximum value for the size of a prezi. However, many years of experience tell us that a prezi can become too large for its own good. A prezi that has too much content will not run smoothly, and may eventually crash. It does not happen often, especially if you stick to the principles for image sizes.

Image sizes

Prezi recommends that you use images with a maximum size of 2800 x 2800 pixels. It is possible to insert images that are larger, but they may prevent your prezi from running smoothly.

If your prezi has images that you do not plan to zoom in on, a size of 1200 x 800 will look beautiful on any computer screen and fill it out without pixelating. Smaller image sizes also work well depending on how close-up you want the image to show.

When inserting a large image file, Prezi sometimes asks if you want to resize the image. If you do not need to zoom into the image, accept the resizing to keep down the size of your prezi. The proposed size for your image will be fine. If you need to zoom into the image when presenting, keep it at its original size.

File types for images

Prezi works with a large number of file types for your images. Each file type has its own characteristic, so check out the following list before you go looking for images.

Interesting image fact: Did you know that all images are actually square in shape?

Look at the cat in the following image. When we insert it on the Prezi canvas and select it, it is easy to see that this image (as with all images) is rectangular in its shape. While the cat is visible, the image background is invisible. This is called transparency when working with images. If the background is not transparent, it is typically white or black. Some file types can use transparency for their background, others cannot. Read on!

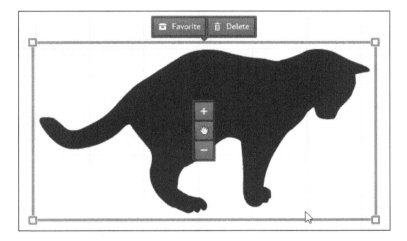

PNG

- ► Commonly used image format for the web
- ► Can use a transparent background

JPG

- ► Commonly used image format for the web
- ► Always has a colored background (background can be white, black, or any other color but will always be present)

GIF

- ▶ Commonly used image format for the web and many other purposes
- ▶ Gif format comes with the option of transparency

SWF

- ▶ Swf files are vector artwork that will not pixelate
- ▶ Swf format comes with transparent backgrounds
- ▶ The use of swf files requires access to a professional image editing program such as Adobe illustrator

PDF

- ▶ Can be used for images and text
- ▶ Pdf is zoom friendly and you can zoom quite close before you see pixelation
- ▶ Contains white background in most cases
- ▶ If your .pdf files have more pages, such as a brochure, it will upload to the canvas as separate pages

Inserting hyperlinks

Prezi is all about sharing information in any form that fits the canvas. With links, you can even share information that is not in Prezi, but located outside of Prezi.

Insert hyperlinks on the Prezi canvas to easily guide the viewers of your prezi to materials and sites that you are referring to in your prezi.

 Inserting a video is also done by inserting links on the canvas. Read *Chapter 10, Media Files in Prezi*, to learn more about inserting videos.

Hyperlinks work as doors that open when clicked, to provide access to websites outside Prezi.

Getting ready

Perform the following instructions to insert a hyperlink:

1. Open a prezi (create a new one or use an existing one).
2. In another browser window, navigate to the address (URL) that you want your viewer to access. We used www.Imprezzing.com.
3. Copy the URL from the address line at the top of the browser window.

How to do it...

1. In your prezi, navigate to the section of the canvas where you want to insert your link.

2. Click on the canvas.

3. In the textbox provided, you can now paste your link.

4. Make sure that the `http://` part is included as shown in the following image:

How it works...

Links in your prezi only work when the presentation is in **Present** mode.

The link is underlined so that it is easily recognized as a link. To use it, just click on it as you would any other link.

There's more...

If you think the link does not look very nice, do as we did in the following image. Make `http://` and `.com` invisible by editing the text so that it has the same color as the background.

 URLs with anything other than HTTP or HTTPS protocols (for example, `ftp://`, `mailto:`, and so on) do not work in Prezi.

3
Symbols and Shapes, Lines and Arrows

In this chapter, we will cover the following recipes:

► Symbols

► Shapes

► Arrows and lines

► Adjusting an arrow/line width

Introduction

Prezi comes with symbols and shapes, a useful collection of simple graphic items that you can easily insert in the canvas. Symbols and shapes provide an easy way to quickly enhance your Prezi.

Symbols are a collection of simple graphic objects; ideal for a quick and simple illustration, or to use as icons. Symbols come in seven styles such as simple dark, simple white, photographic, sketched, cute, etched, and stickers. The style groups do not offer different objects; mostly they offer the same objects, but rendered in different styles.

Symbols are vector graphics. Images in the vector format can be scaled to any size without loss of quality. This means that you can use and adjust symbols to any size on the canvas: small, medium, or large. Use the symbols for anything from icons (small on the canvas) to imagery that you zoom into (big on the canvas).

Shapes are a collection of geometrical shapes (rectangles, triangles, and circles) that are useful for a variety of purposes, for simple decoration, use as icons, or as an alternative to frames (as a background for text or objects).

Lines and arrows are objects that you can easily draw with a click of your mouse. They are great tools to structure your Prezi and direct attention to specific areas.

[Shapes, Lines, and Arrows are all subject to a limited color palette.]

Symbols

Symbols provide easy access to professionally designed icons that are useful in many situations. Symbols are simple, yet beautiful. They can quickly become your go-to option for here and now access to professional graphics that just work.

Getting ready

Symbols range in look from cool or cute to professional and clean, so begin by checking out the various styles. Decide which style best fits your purpose.

[Choosing the same style for all your symbols in a Prezi will help you obtain a uniform style for your Prezi.]

How to do it...

1. Go to the **Insert** menu.
2. Choose **Symbols & Shapes**.
3. Click on the **Styles** category that you want for your symbol.
4. Click on the symbol that you want to use.
5. Grab it and drag it onto the canvas.
6. Drop the symbol where you want it.

Prezi offers quick access to symbols and shapes in various styles as shown in the following screenshot:

How it works...

Once the symbol is placed on the canvas, select it to adjust its placement, size, and angle.

It is not possible to change the coloring of a symbol.

If you decide that you do not want it after all, just click to select the symbol and hit *Delete* on your keyboard or on the toolbar on top of the selected item, as shown in the following screenshot:

There's more...

Inserting a lot of symbols (or shapes) will sometimes make your Prezi heavy, in the sense that it takes more time to update, does not run smoothly in present mode, and may eventually crash. These are unwanted effects of inserting too many symbols or shapes. The only way to avoid this is to remove some of the symbols or shapes, until your Prezi responds normally to your updates and commands.

There is no set number for how many symbols (or shapes) you can safely insert in a Prezi. This all depends on how much other stuff you have on the canvas.

 If you have multiple symbols (or shapes) in your Prezi, be aware that they may cause your Prezi to look too cluttered and unprofessional.

Shapes

Shapes is a collection of rectangles, circles, and triangles that you can easily insert in the canvas. They can be used for many purposes, such as serving as background for text or other content. They also work well for decoration purposes, either as they are or combined into whatever pattern or structure you like.

How to do it...

1. Go to the **Insert** menu.
2. Choose **Symbols & Shapes** to open the **Shapes** category.
3. Click on the shape you want.
4. Grab it and drag it onto the canvas.
5. Drop the shape where you want it.

Simple geometrical shapes are found in the bottom right of this menu, as shown in the following screenshot:

How it works...

Once the shape is placed on the canvas, select it to adjust its placement, size, and angle. Note that by dragging an edge of a selected square shape or triangle shape, you can adjust the proportions of this shape.

There's more...

When you access the **Shapes** panel, the shapes are shown as blue or white. Once you insert the shape on your canvas, its color will be different from what it was in the panel. This is due to the fact that it is the underlying Prezi template and color themes that control the color scheme for **Shapes**.

Therefore, the shapes you select will be colored according to the template you chose. Shapes are all blue and white when shown in the **Shapes** panel in the following screenshot:

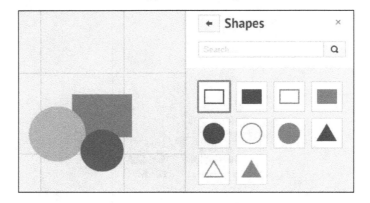

Changing the color of a shape

The colors of **Shapes** are controlled by the template and color theme behind your Prezi. The benefit of this is that all the colors match beautifully. Still, sometimes you might want another color for your shape than the preset color.

Fortunately, this is easy to do with the small toolbar that appears on selecting the image. Use it to choose and apply a color from a matching mini palette.

Click on **Style** on the toolbar to access the color choices. **Style** on the black toolbar offers color choices that match your template, as shown in the following screenshot:

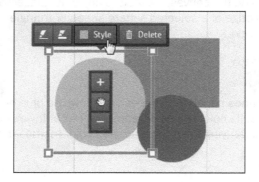

The great advantage of using this tool is that all the color choices offered to you will match the colors in your Prezi's template and theme. Take a look at the icon shown in the following screenshot:

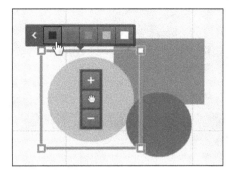

 The color choices in the small palette are controlled by your Prezi template. It is not possible to alter or edit the palette for a template.

See also

▶ Read more about colors in *Chapter 11, Templates, Colors, and Fonts.*

Arrows and lines

Prezi includes arrows and lines that are attractive and useful for many purposes. You can easily adjust the color and length of an arrow or line to make it fit your purpose.

How to do it...

1. Go to the **Insert** menu.
2. Choose **Draw arrow** or **Draw line**.
3. Place the cursor on the canvas where you want your arrow/line to begin.
4. Holding the left mouse button down, drag to where you want the arrow/line to end.
5. Let go of the mouse button when your arrow/line is long enough.

Take a look at the drop-down menu shown in the following screenshot:

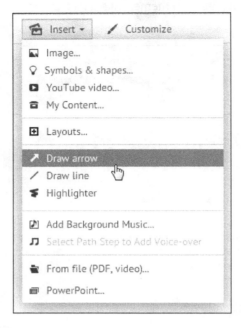

How it works...

Once the arrow/line is on the canvas, you can adjust its placement, length, width, curvature, and direction.

Selecting the arrow/line produces three square handles on the arrow/line. Use these handles to adjust the length and curvature of the arrow/line. Take a look at the arrow shown in the following screenshot:

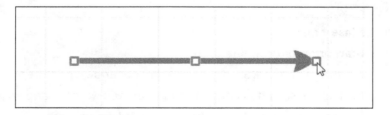

Task to be done	How to do it
To adjust direction	Drag an end of the square handle
To adjust length	Drag an end of the square handle
To adjust curvature	Drag the middle square handle

Changing the color of an arrow/line

It is possible to change the color of an arrow/line. To do so, select the arrow/line and choose **Style** on the small menu that appears above the arrow/line, as shown in the following screenshot:

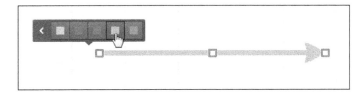

The color choices on the mini palette are controlled by the applied template or color theme.

[The color choices in the mini palette cannot be changed without changing the color theme.]

Adjusting arrow/line width

It is possible to change the width of an arrow/line. To do so, select the arrow/line and choose one of the pencil icons to the left on the small menu that appears above the arrow/line.

How to do it...

1. Select the arrow/line whose width you want to change.
2. Click on the pencil icon to the left.
3. For a thinner arrow/line, choose pencil icon **1**.
4. For a thicker arrow/line, choose pencil icon **2**.
5. Clicking 1 or 2 several times will re-apply the effect.

Use the pencil icons to make your arrow/line thinner or thicker as shown in the following screenshot:

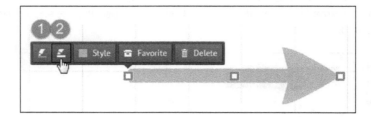

If you need to create arrows/lines of the same size and thickness, duplication (*Ctrl + D*) is an easy way to create multiple identical arrows/lines.

4
Editing Elements on the Canvas

In this chapter, we will cover the following recipes:

- ▸ Moving an element (image, text, or other type)
- ▸ Rotating an element
- ▸ Resizing an element
- ▸ Adjusting text elements to an equal size
- ▸ Adjusting elements to the same turn degree
- ▸ Selecting multiple elements
- ▸ Grouping and un-grouping elements
- ▸ Working in layers

Introduction

When we work in Prezi, we insert many different kinds of material on the canvas. We write texts, insert images, use videos, frames, and other elements.

As a means to refer to all these different kinds of materials as a group, we will use the term "elements", thus referring, in general, to various materials that we use and insert into Prezi.

This chapter covers how to work with elements on your canvas. You will learn how to resize, turn, move, group, and layer various kinds of elements.

The processes of re-sizing, turning, moving, grouping, and layering are the same for all elements, whether it is a text element, an image, a group, or any other type.

In a typical prezi design process, you will use all these functions a lot.

Taking time to familiarize yourself with all the principles in this chapter will save you a lot of time in the long run, by making your prezi design process more efficient and easier.

Moving an element – image, text, or some other type

No matter how much time you spend planning your design before you begin working on the Prezi canvas, you will find that you will often need to move texts, images, and other elements to different positions on the canvas.

Sometimes the moves will be big; at other times, you will just want to fine-tune an element's position.

Fortunately, Prezi makes it easy. For any kind of element, there are two ways to do the big moves, and one for the incremental adjustments.

Let's begin with the big moves.

How to do it...

1. Using your mouse, click on an element to select it.
2. Hold your left mouse button down.
3. Now move the element by dragging the mouse.
4. Release the mouse button when the element is at the desired place on your canvas.

Alternatively, you can use the following method:

1. Using your mouse, click on an element to select it.
2. Grab the hand icon in the middle of the black toolbar on the element.
3. Hold and drag the selected element on the canvas, as shown in the following screenshot:

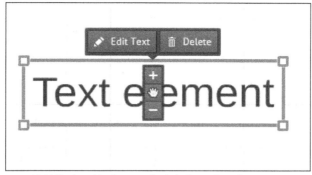

Hold the hand to drag a selected element on the canvas

For the smaller or incremental adjustments in position, we can use the arrow keys on your keyboard, which is the easiest way:

1. Using your mouse, click on an element to select it.

2. Use your left or right arrow key on the keyboard, as shown in the following figure, to "nudge" the selected element into place:

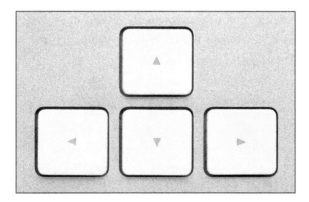

Note that there are two settings to move the selected elements using the arrow keys:

1. Clicking on an arrow key moves a selected element by 1 pixel.

2. Clicking on an arrow key while holding down *Shift* moves a selected element by 10 pixels.

There's more...

Dragging an element to the edge of the visible part of the canvas will scroll the canvas to make room for the element.

Rotating an element

One of the cool things about Prezi is that you can angle or turn any element on the canvas, so that it is in a turned position. When shown in the **Present** mode, Prezi turns the canvas to show the element as it is (meaning its original, upright look), thus creating the illusion that the element turns.

Turning is a very characteristic Prezi feature. However, at the same time, it is a feature that you should use with caution. Turning can make your audience feel seasick, if your canvas turns around too much or too frequently.

How to do it...

Turning adds a great variety to Prezi when used right. It is beautiful to look at, and a feature that we wouldn't find in any other presentation program.

To rotate an element, you will need to use your mouse and perform the following steps:

1. Click on the element to select it.
2. The selected element now has a blue frame around it.
3. Hover your mouse over one of the corners of the blue frame.
4. A lever with a circle will be displayed.
5. Hold and drag the lever to rotate the element.

In the following screenshot, the element to the left is upright, and to the right, we see the element when rotated:

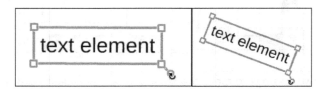

Resizing an element

No matter how much time you spend planning your design before you begin working on the Prezi canvas, you will often need to adjust the size of texts, images, and other elements, so that they fit your purpose better.

Fortunately, Prezi makes it easy! Just grab your mouse and follow along.

1. Click on the element to select it.
2. The blue frame is now visible.
3. Click and hold one of the square corner markers of the blue frame.
4. Drag to adjust the element size.

Drag the square corner marker to adjust the size of a selected element, as shown in the following screenshot:

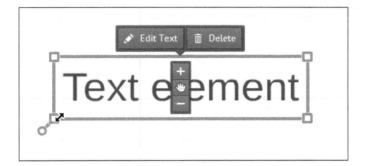

Adjusting text elements to the same size

Some text elements of the same kind (headers are an example) need to be of equal size. When a text element that you are working with has just the right size for your needs, you can adjust other text elements so that they have the same size.

Prezi can help you do this.

Getting ready

Create two text elements (elements 1 and 2). Adjust the size of element 1 so that it is larger than element 2. We will now use Prezi to help us re-size element 2 to have the exact same size as element 1.

Make sure both elements are visible as you work to adjust the size.

How to do it...

1. Click on element 2 to select it.

2. Notice the blue selection frame around it. Click and drag one of the square corner markers to adjust the size of this text element.

3. As you resize, you will notice that text element 1 is sometimes encompassed by a thinner blue frame (as shown in the following image). The thin blue frame indicates that the elements now have the same size.

In the following screenshot, as we resize text element 2, text element 1 is highlighted by a thin blue frame when sizes correspond:

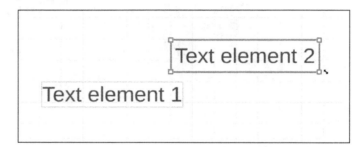

Adjusting elements to the same turn degree

Consistency helps your audience understand your presentation. For this reason, you want elements of the same type (such as headings, subheadings, details, and so on) to look the same.

Let's say a header on your canvas is turned just the way you like it. In this case, you want your other headings (sub-headings, details, and so on) to turn in the exact same way.

Prezi can help you easily adjust text elements so that they are turned to the same angle.

Getting ready

Decide which of your elements is turned to the right angle. We'll call this "element 1". Now work with the element that you want to adjust (element 2) to have an identical angle as element 1.

Make sure both elements are visible on the canvas as you work.

How to do it...

1. Click on element 2 to select it (the one that you want to adjust).

2. Notice the blue frame around the element.

3. Hovering over a square corner marker activates a round turn-lever.

4. Drag the lever and notice that element 1 is encompassed by a thinner blue frame when the angling is the same for the two elements, as shown in the following screenshot:

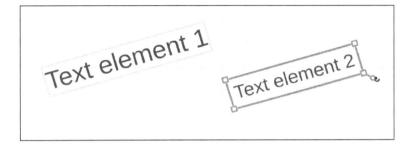

 If you are too close or too far from an element, selecting can be difficult. Try zooming in or out to adjust to a zoom level that lets you select the element in question (zoom out for large elements and zoom in for small ones).

Selecting multiple elements

In the process of designing a Prezi, you will often need to perform changes such as resizing, angling, or moving multiple elements at one time. When you have many elements on your canvas, it is time consuming to edit each one separately.

The good news is that you can add changes to multiple elements in one operation, thus saving you loads of time and effort.

There are two different ways to select multiple elements. One is called click-selecting. The other method is known as marquee-selecting because we drag a "marquee" around the selected elements. We will look at both methods.

Click-selecting multiple elements

Selecting multiple individual elements by click-selecting is especially useful when you want to edit elements that are located in different places on your canvas.

Getting ready

If the elements that you need to select are widely spread out, click on the house icon (found when you hover the mouse on the right side of the canvas) for a complete overview of all elements on your canvas.

How to do it...

1. Make sure nothing is selected.
2. Hold down the *Shift* key.
3. Click on the elements you want to select, one by one.
4. The selected elements now have a collective blue box line around them.
5. Use a square marker in a corner of the box to resize or turn the selected elements.

In the following screenshot, a thin blue box line encompasses the selected elements:

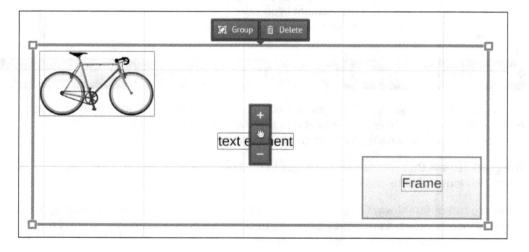

 Changing multiple elements in one operation allows you to maintain the original proportions in the size of the various elements.

Marquee-selecting multiple elements

As an alternative to selecting multiple elements by clicking on each element individually, the marquee-selection, where you drag your mouse over multiple elements to select them, is often faster.

Getting ready

Remember that a marquee-selection will select all elements included in the marquee area.

The marquee method selects elements in a square area (see the following figure). Any elements that you do not want included by the marquee-selection should be moved out of this area before you begin.

How to do it...

1. Hold down the *Shift* key on your keyboard.
2. Position your mouse by the top-left element that you want to select.
3. Click, hold, and drag the mouse diagonally towards the right and down.
4. The marquee area is encompassed by a thin black line.
5. Keep dragging your mouse until all elements are included in the marquee square.
6. Let go of the mouse button and then release the *Shift* key.
7. The blue selection frame is now visible. Use it to resize, angle, or move all the selected elements.

In the following screenshot, we have marquee-selected text element and a picture:

Grouping and ungrouping elements

Sometimes you know that you want to keep certain elements together as they are shown on your canvas right now. This could be an image of a tree that you adjusted and put in front of an image of a house. In Prezi, we can glue elements together by creating a group.

When elements have been grouped, they will be edited as one. This means that they keep their relative position and size when you move, resize, or turn the group on the canvas.

A group will exist until you choose to ungroup it.

Getting ready

Make sure that the elements that you want in the group are placed where you want them to be. Check that each one has the size that you want it to have. Grouped elements cannot be edited individually. (To edit individually, you would need to ungroup the elements).

How to do it...

1. Make sure nothing is selected.
2. Hold down the *Shift* key on your keyboard.
3. Now select multiple elements by clicking on each element individually, or by applying the marquee-selection (for marquee-selection, please refer to the preceding recipe).
4. We selected the text and the Post-it note. This is indicated by the blue selection box as shown in the following picture.
5. Click on **Group** in the black toolbox above the selection box.

A group is one single element because the (previous) single elements are now glued together. Make a group of multiple selected elements by clicking on **Group**, as shown in the following screenshot:

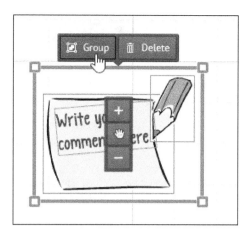

Ungrouping elements

Ungrouping is very straight forward and easy to do.

How to do it...

1. Click on the group to select it.
2. Click on **Ungroup** on the toolbar above the selection box, as shown in the following screenshot:

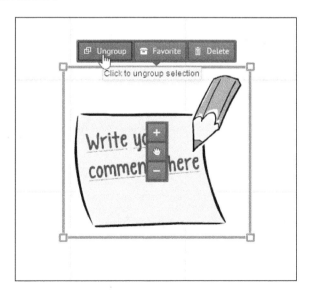

Now the items are no longer grouped and can be edited individually.

Working in layers

The Prezi canvas is made up of an infinite number of layers. While you cannot see the layers themselves, all elements (frames, images, texts, and everything else) on the canvas are actually placed in a separate layer. Consequently, all elements are in their own layer.

Working in layers is very much like creating a layered cake; the first element (frames, images, texts, and everything else) you add is placed in the bottom layer, the next one is placed in the layer above the first one, and so forth.

If two or more elements are placed in their own area of the canvas, we cannot see the layering. However, try placing an element in the exact same area as an existing element and you will notice that one element is on top of the other (fully or partially). The element on top will be the one that was inserted at a later point in time than the element below it (much like the icing on top of the cake that comes on last).

Getting ready

When an element is added to the canvas, we may need to change the element's position in order to make it look nicer, or to prevent it from blocking the view of the items below it.

In the following image, the order of the heart and the text needs to be changed:

Fortunately, it is easy to adjust the order that our elements have on the canvas.

How to do it...

Elements can be moved to control which elements are on top or below.

1. Right-click on the element that you want to move to a different layer.
2. On right-click, the menu opens.

3. In this menu, choose **Bring Forward** to move the element one layer upwards or **Bring to Front** to bring the element all the way to the top layer.

4. To move downwards, choose **Send Backward** to move the element downwards or **Send to Back** to move the element all the way to the bottom layer.

In the following screenshot, we want to move the speech bubble forward:

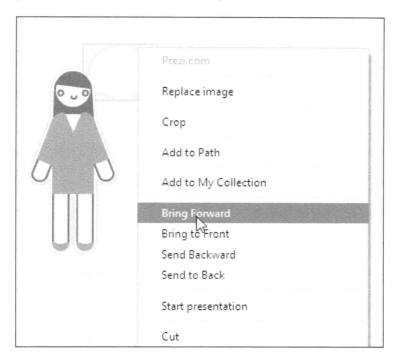

There's more...

In order to move several elements collectively to another layer, you can group the elements. A group is treated by Prezi as one single element, and can be moved backwards or forwards in the layer order as any other element.

5
Path and Steps

In this chapter, we will cover the following recipes:

- ▶ Setting steps to create a path
- ▶ Creating steps using frames and elements
- ▶ Path order
- ▶ Editing steps
- ▶ Adding additional steps using the canvas
- ▶ Rearranging steps using the canvas
- ▶ Deleting steps using the canvas
- ▶ Rearranging steps using the path lane
- ▶ Deleting steps using the path lane
- ▶ Path lane quick tools: Adding the current view
- ▶ Path lane quick tools: Clear all option

Introduction

Prezi's working space or background is called the canvas. Everything we want in the prezi must be added to the canvas.

When we switch to **Present** mode, we want our prezi to show the elements on the canvas in a specific order, much like setting an order for your slides in a PowerPoint presentation. We do this by creating steps. After creating steps, we make sure our steps appear in the order we want. Creating this order is referred to as creating a path. It is somewhat like setting a route for a bus, in the sense that the path is the route that your audience will follow through the material on your canvas.

This chapter tells you how to create steps, and how to create and edit a path in Prezi.

Elements that can be used as steps are anything that you can put on the canvas; texts, image, videos, symbols, shapes, grouped elements, PDFs, and so on.

In that sense, frames too are elements, and can be used as steps. However, frames play a number of different roles on the canvas, so we need to refer to them as a separate group. For this reason, we operate with elements and frames as two separate categories, even if there is a huge overlap.

If you are not quite sure of the role that frames play when adding elements to your path, please refer to *Chapter 6, Frames and Prezi Ratio*.

 You do not have to assign all elements on the canvas to the path. Sometimes it can be nice to keep items at hand as extra information or just because it looks good as part of your design.

Setting steps to create a path

On the Prezi screen is an area to the left that we have not yet used—the grey panel. This small grey area includes some of the features that are key factors of the Prezi magic, as this is where we set the route for our "passengers" (that is, the audience) for their ride through our Prezi presentation. In other words, this grey panel to the left is dedicated to working with your path.

To access the features in the path lane in order to create or edit your path, you must be in **Edit Path** mode.

You activate edit path mode by clicking on **Edit Path** in the lower-left corner of the Prezi screen, as shown in the following screenshot:

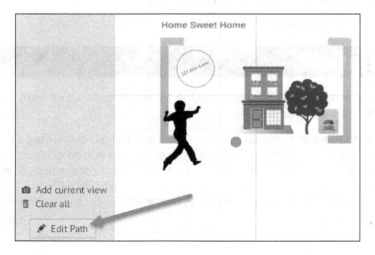

Getting ready

If you want to use these recipes as an exercise, we suggest that you prepare by making sure of the following:

1. Work with at least five elements on the canvas.

2. Make sure your prezi has no path (if you need to clear your path, switch to **path mode** and click on **Clear All** at the bottom of the path lane).

3. At least one image is placed in a frame.

How to do it...

1. Open the prezi that you want to work in.

2. Switch to edit path mode by clicking on **Edit Path**.

3. One by one, click on the elements that you want to add to the path.

4. Check the path lane to see your elements represented by thumbnails.

In the following screenshot, the steps we created are shown in the path lane as thumbnails:

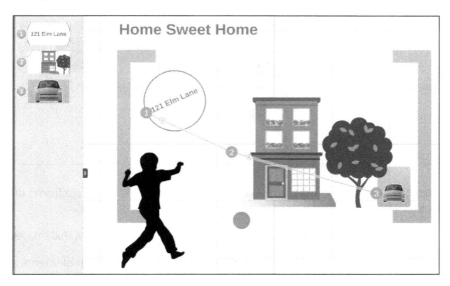

How it works...

To create this path, we first selected the circle frame that holds the street name, and Prezi added it to the path. Next, we selected the house and Prezi added it to the path. Finally, the yellow car was selected and added.

The element that was selected first is placed at the top of the path lane. Every element that is added is inserted subsequently.

Creating steps using frames and elements

Be aware that it often makes a big difference whether you choose to create your step on an element, or on a frame that holds this element.

In the preceding screenshot, the **121 Elm Lane** text element and the image of the yellow car are both used as steps. The frames that surround them are not used as steps.

To show you the difference, we will now add two more steps to our path. These steps will be based on the two frames that hold the street name and the car, respectively. Take a look at the following screenshot:

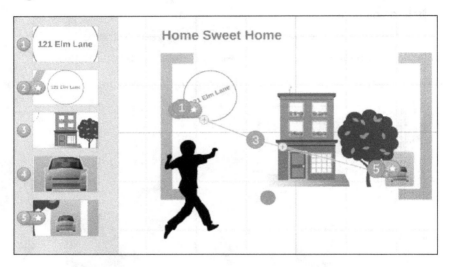

In the preceding screenshot, step 1 is a text element and step 2 is the circle frame around this element.

Step 4 is the image of the car and step 5 is the rectangle frame that holds this image.

As you can clearly see, there is a big difference between creating steps on elements and on frames.

One is not better or more correct than the other. Sometimes you need a step to be an element. This element can be in a frame or by itself. At other times, you need the step to be a frame in order to show the frame and its content.

See also

Frames are a huge topic in Prezi. To learn more about frames, we suggest that you take a look at *Chapter 6, Frames* and Prezi Ratio, *Chapter 12, Presenting with Prezi, Appendix A, Design,* and *Appendix B, Transitions.*

Furthermore, if you look at step 2 in the path lane in the preceding image, notice that even if the text is angled on the canvas, it is not angled in the path lane. This is a perfect example of the fact that Prezi shows everything right way up. Read more about this in *Chapter 7, Zoom and Turn.*

The path order

When you are in **Edit Path** mode, the path you set is shown on the canvas as a thin blue line.

This line, the path, goes from element to element, following the order in which you created the steps. The number in the small blue circle to the left of the steps shows the step number that is currently assigned to this element/frame.

When you click on **Present** to switch to present mode, this is the order Prezi will use to move forward through your material. Please refer to the image in the *How to do it...* section of the *Setting steps to create a path* recipe; the order of your steps is shown by a thin blue line and blue number circles in edit path mode.

Editing steps

Editing your steps mainly means one of these three actions:

- ▶ Adding additional steps to your path
- ▶ Rearranging the order of steps
- ▶ Deleting steps

There are two places you can go to edit your steps: the canvas (the main working area in the center with all the elements) and the path lane (the thumbnails in the left grey column).

Because you have the most editing options on the canvas, this is where you will be doing the major part of the editing of steps. On the canvas, it is easy to add new steps and make the bigger adjustments to your path order.

The path lane does not offer as many options. However, it does provide quick and easy access to a few main features that you will likely use a lot. In the path lane, it is easy to move one or two steps to new positions in the order. Deleting steps is a breeze here too.

Adding an element to the path lane means the exact same thing as creating a step. It is easy when you think about it. Steps are the only thing you will ever find in the path lane.

Adding additional steps using the canvas

Take a look at the following screenshot. We will work with the steps in this picture to show you how you can edit and add steps to an existing path.

In this process, it is very useful to keep an eye on the receiving element. In the process of assigning a path step to an element, when hovering over this with your mouse, look for the thin blue frame that indicates that this frame is selected.

To learn how to begin creating a path, please read the *Setting steps to create a path* section and refer to the image in the *How to do it...* section.

As it is clearly seen in the path lane (thumbnails) and on the canvas (number circles), this prezi has three steps already. Now we want to add more steps.

How to do it...

In this section, we show you how to add steps to an existing path:

1. Use a prezi that has multiple elements on the canvas as well as an existing path.
2. Click on **Edit Path** to switch to path mode.

Now the path lane and path are visible. Take a close look at your path (or ours in the preceding image). Notice that there are two kinds of circles on the path lane: the number circles (showing the step number for an element) and the smaller circles that have a plus sign in them.

The plus-circles provide an easy way to create new steps in your Prezi:

1. In the preceding image, we click and drag the plus-circle that follows the step 2 circle (the house).
2. We are going to drop this plus-circle on the image of the boy. Hover your mouse over the boy and drop the plus-circle when you see the image surrounded by a thin blue frame:

Number circles are followed by a plus-circle on the path lane. The last step does not offer a plus-circle. A step that you create with a plus-circle joins the path right after the number-circle that it adheres to. Take a look at the following screenshot:

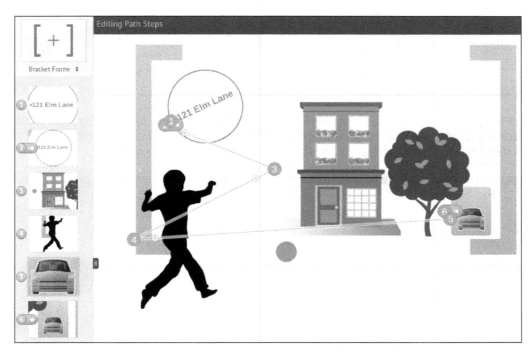

Here the boy is step 4, just after the house (step 3). Consequently, the car is now step 5.

As you may have noticed, there is still a plus-circle after the number-circle at step 2. We can create more steps to follow step 2.

With the plus-circle feature, Prezi makes it easy to add as many steps to a presentation as you want to, and to place them exactly in the order you want.

Rearranging steps using the canvas

Most times when we are working in Prezi, we are constantly editing our content. More often than not, creating a prezi involves switching back and forth between developing new ideas, adding new content, and editing the existing content.

As a result, you will often need to adjust the order of steps so that your Prezi reflects your ideas of today, rather than what you were thinking last week.

We'll show you how easy it is to switch your steps on an existing path. Please refer to the image in the *How to do it...* section of the *Setting steps to create a path* recipe. Here, we are in **Edit path** mode in order to rearrange steps on the canvas.

Getting ready

In this section, we show you how to rearrange steps on an existing path. Perform the following steps:

1. Use a prezi that has multiple elements on the canvas as well as a path.
2. Click on **Edit Path** to switch to path mode.

Now the path is visible. Take a close look at your path (or ours in the preceding image). Notice that every single step has a circle with a number in it. We call these number-circles. The number-circle for a step shows this step's number in the order on the path.

Dragging the number-circle to another element is an easy way to rearrange the order of steps.

Here, we want to make the title "Home Sweet Home" the first step for our prezi, as shown in the following screenshot:

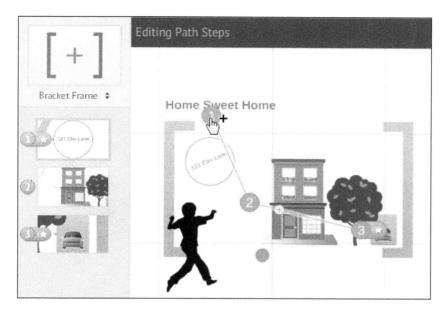

How to do it...

1. Using the mouse, click and hold the number-circle that you want to move in order to assign it to a different element.

2. Drag it to the element that you want to assign it to (the title).

3. Hover over this element until it is highlighted.

4. When highlighted, drop the number-circle on the new element, as shown in the following screenshot:

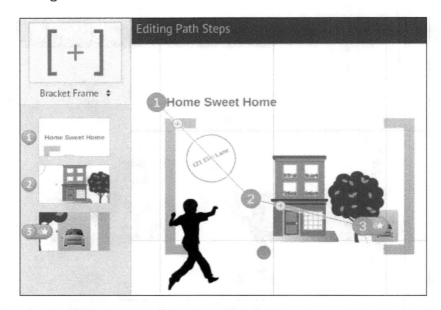

Deleting steps using the canvas

Developing a presentation is almost an organic process. The presentation keeps growing as you add materials and develop your ideas on the canvas. Eventually, you may need to delete steps from your prezi path.

Deleting a step from the prezi path can mean two different scenarios. In both cases, we are looking at an element that is a step on the path.

Scenario 1: Deleting the element from the canvas means that it will also disappear from the path.

Scenario 2: Deleting the step (by deleting the number-circle or using the red circle in the path lane) means that your item is still on the canvas, but you chose not to use it as a step. (Compare to a bus driving by a building instead of stopping.)

Sometimes it is nice to keep material on your canvas without using it as a step. You may want to have it at hand as extra information or just because it looks good as part of your design.

In this section, we show you how to keep content on the canvas, even if you remove it from the path.

Getting ready

In this section, we show you how to delete steps from a path without deleting the content. Take a look at the following steps:

1. Open a prezi that has multiple elements on the canvas as well as a path.
2. Click on **Edit Path** to switch to path mode.

Now the path lane and path are visible.

How to do it...

1. On the canvas, locate the number-circle that is associated with the step that you want to delete.
2. Using your mouse, hold and drag the number-circle to an empty spot on the canvas or anywhere outside the grey border around the canvas.
3. Drop the number-circle here by releasing your mouse.

Voila! The step is deleted:

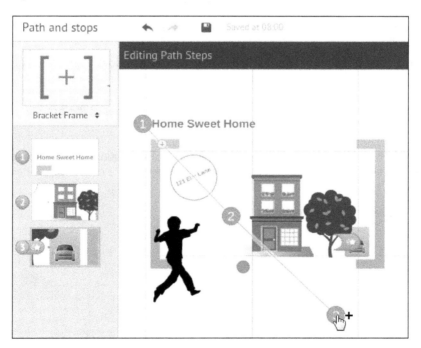

Rearranging steps using the path lane

For most prezi users, the process of creating a prezi inevitably includes a large number of edits. Even if you spend a lot of time planning your prezi, you will need to rearrange some steps. Fortunately, the path lane makes it easy.

Getting ready

In the path lane, it is very easy to move a step to a new position. To do so, perform the following steps:

1. Open a prezi that has multiple elements on the canvas as well as a path.
2. Click on **Edit Path** to switch to path mode.

Now the path lane is visible on the left side of your screen.

How to do it...

To move a step in the path lane, here is what you do:

1. In the path lane, locate the step that you want at another position in the order of steps.
2. Using your mouse, hold and drag this step upwards or downwards to its new position.
3. Drop the step here by releasing your mouse.

The step is now located at a different another position in the order of the path.

[If you used to work in PowerPoint for your presentations, thinking of steps as slides might help you understand this easily.]

Take a look at the following screenshot:

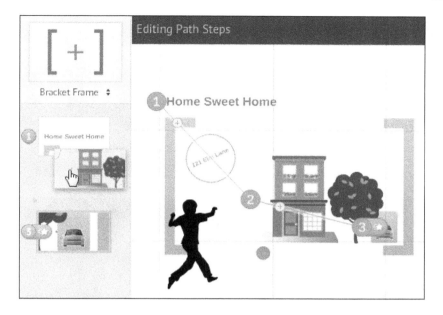

[Because you can only move one step at a time using the
path lane, the canvas works better for edits that include
multiple steps.]

Deleting steps using the path lane

Creating a Prezi is a creative process. As in any creative process, we will sometimes need to
edit our design ideas, remove material, or delete steps.

In this recipe, we remove steps from the path by using features in the path lane.

Getting ready

This recipe shows you how easy it is to delete a single step with just a click. Perform the
following steps on your prezi:

1. Open a prezi that has multiple elements on the canvas as well as a path.
2. Click on **Edit Path** to switch to path mode.

Now the path lane is visible on the left side of your screen.

How to do it...

To delete a step in the path lane, here is what you do:

1. In the path lane, locate the thumbnail for the step that you want to delete.
2. Using your mouse, hover over the thumbnail for this step.
3. Notice the red circle that appears in the top-right corner.
4. Clicking on the red circle removes the thumbnail and deletes this step.

Take a look at the following screenshot:

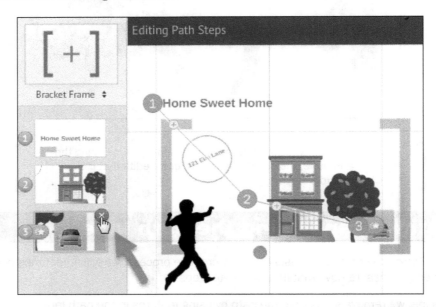

Path lane quick tools – Adding current view

At the very bottom of the path lane (after clicking on the **Edit Path** button), we find these two options: **Add current view** and **Clear all**:

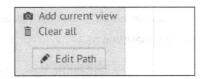

Add current view provides a quick way to create a single step based on what is currently showing on your screen. When you click on **Add current view**, Prezi adds an invisible frame to your canvas and also adds it to your path lane.

The **Clear all** command provides a fast way to clear your path lane by deleting all the existing steps. If **Clear all** is selected accidentally, *Ctrl + Z* brings the path back.

Read the following two recipes to learn how to use these great features.

Getting ready

To create a step using **Add current view**, here is what you do:

1. Open a prezi that has some kind of content on the canvas.
2. Click on **Edit Path** to switch to path mode.

Now the path lane is visible on the left side of your screen.

How to do it...

1. Adjust the size (zoom level) and placement of the canvas, so that the screen shows the section that you want to see.
2. Hover over **Add current view** at the bottom of the path lane.
3. Click on **Add current view**.
4. With this click, the frame is created on the canvas and added as a step to the path lane.

 When you click on **Add current view**, the frame that is created adheres to your prezi's frame ratio (provided you set it). The ratio will be reflected by the proportions of the frame as well as the grey "masking" areas around the frame (Refer to *Chapter 6, Frames and Prezi Ratio*, to learn more about frame ratio.)

Path lane quick tools – the Clear all option

Clear all is the fastest way to clear your path completely of all steps. In cases where you are experimenting or your Prezi has changed a lot since you started, we think you will find that it is a very useful tool.

Getting ready

To delete all steps in your path lane using **Clear all**, here is what you need to do:

1. Open a prezi that has content on the canvas and a path.
2. Click on **Edit Path** to switch to path mode.

Now the path lane is visible on the left side of your screen.

How to do it...

1. Locate the **Clear all** button at the bottom of the path lane.
2. Click on it to delete all the steps.

Your steps are now deleted and you can begin creating new steps.

Clear all deletes steps and does not impact the content on the canvas. If **Clear all** is selected accidentally, *Ctrl + Z* brings the path back.

6
Frames and Prezi Ratio

In this chapter, we will cover the following recipes:

- ► What are frames used for?
- ► Types of frames
- ► Inserting frames
- ► How do frames work?
- ► Content in a frame
- ► Removing content from a frame
- ► Adjusting the size of a frame
- ► Turning a frame
- ► Moving a frame
- ► Editing a frame without impacting content
- ► The frame toolbar
- ► Deleting a frame (overview)
- ► Prezi ratio

Introduction

Prezi's working space or background is called the canvas. Everything we want in the prezi must be added to the canvas. When we work in Prezi, we insert many kinds of material onto the canvas, such as texts, images, videos, frames, and other elements.

As a means to refer to all these different kinds of materials as a group, we will use the term **elements**, thus referring to various materials that we use and insert in Prezi.

We can add elements of all kinds on to the canvas and place them where we see fit. Once our elements are on the canvas, we set our presentation to move forward from one element to another by adding each element to the path lane. This process is referred to as creating steps. The order of our steps defines how our prezi advances in **Present** mode.

An element that is set as a step automatically fills our screen when we reach it (in **Present** mode). Sometimes this is what we want; at other times we want a different look. We may want space around an element. We may want to combine elements or proceed in a specific way through our material. For these purposes, we need frames.

Most prezis will be viewed on a device that is either 16:9 or 4:3 in its screen proportion; this can be a 16:9 computer screen or a 4:3 projector. In this chapter, you will learn how to set the overall ratio for your prezi, and we show you how this setting reflects on your frames so that they automatically match the required screen proportions.

This book offers three different sections about frames. This chapter describes how frames work—you might call it the mechanics. *Appendix A*, *Design*, and *Appendix B*, *Transitions*, focus on how to use frames as part of the creative outlay for your prezi. We suggest that you familiarize yourself with the mechanics before you start thinking about design and creative uses for frames.

If you are not familiar with path and steps, *Chapter 5*, *Path and Steps*, will get you there! Need to refresh your memory of the canvas? Read *Chapter 2*, *Inserting Text, Images, and Links*.

What are frames used for?

Frames are an integral part of how prezi works. We use them all the time to group and organize content, for decoration purposes, and to control how the content is presented when we switch to **Present** mode.

Remember that any element (frame, image, text element, or any other) that we show as a step in our prezi will fill the entire screen. Let's consider, as an example, an image of a car. Added as a step, the car will fill the screen in **Present** mode. However, if the car is put in a frame, and you use the frame as a path step, it will be the frame that fills the screen. The element in the frame can now be resized to be shown at any size, large, small, or partly as you please.

Frames in Prezi are used to control in detail what a path step looks like in **Present** mode. In other words, it is the use of frames that allows us to adjust what is shown in a step and how it is shown.

The core of using frames is that they allow us to control exactly which section of the canvas is shown in a step.

This use of frames is a key factor of how to create the look and feel that is so characteristic of Prezi.

Read on and learn how to create steps that show details, overviews, and everything in between.

Types of frames

Prezi offers four kinds of frames. They are as follows:

- ▸ Bracket frame
- ▸ Circle frame
- ▸ Rectangle frame
- ▸ Invisible frame

As you may have guessed from their names, the frames look different in shape, color scheme, and visibility. However, in spite of this, they work in the exact same way. This is great, because it means that if you understand how to handle the circle frame, you will also know how to handle the other frames.

However, because the invisible frame is invisible, it never conflicts with your design style or elements on the canvas. For that reason, the invisible frame is by far the frame that is used most in Prezi.

Please refer to *Appendix A*, *Design*, and *Appendix B*, *Transitions*, to learn more about how to use frames as part of your design tool box.

Inserting frames

It is easy to insert frames onto the canvas. All frame types are inserted in the same way: first you select the type of frame and then you insert it.

For both of these steps, you will be working in the top-left corner of the Prezi user interface.

As shown in the following screenshot, right-click below the **Bracket Frame** icon to open the drop-down menu showing the various frame types:

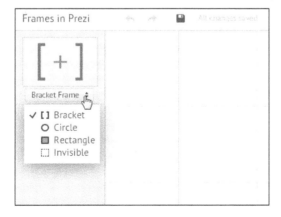

How to do it...

1. On the drop-down menu, choose the frame type that you want to insert on the canvas by clicking on it.

2. Insert the frame onto the canvas by either clicking on the frame icon with the **+** sign or by dragging it onto the canvas.

3. Note that the frame is automatically added to the path as a step.

How do frames work?

To help you understand how the frames work, we have created two examples. The first example uses an image as a step (no frames).The second example uses a frame around an image as a step.

We suggest that you study or execute both examples (it's a five minute exercise). Comparing the two will help you easily grasp how frames work and why they are a key element in any prezi.

How to do it...

Example 1: A path step that does not use frames:

1. Begin by opening the prezi that you want to work in.

2. Search the Internet or your computer for an image (we are using a house, but any image will do).

3. Insert the image onto the canvas.

4. Click on **Edit Path** to switch to path mode.

5. Click on the image to add it to the path.

6. To make this image step number one, you may have to drag it to the top of the path lane.

7. Click on **Present** to see your step in present mode.

Our image was added to the path as a step and is shown in the following screenshot in **Present** mode:

Now we have created a step that is based on the image file. The image fills the screen in present mode.

Example 2: A path step that uses a frame as the step:

1. Use the same prezi and image as in example 1 (if you wish to continue after example 1, use *Esc* to switch from **Present** mode to **Edit** mode).
2. On the drop-down menu in the top-left corner, choose the frame type that you want to insert on the canvas by clicking on it. (We use the bracket frame, but any frame will work.)
3. Insert the frame onto the canvas by either clicking on the frame icon with the **+** sign or dragging it onto the canvas.
4. Note that the frame is automatically added to the path as a step.
5. To make this image step number two, you may have to drag it upwards in the path lane.
6. Click on **Present** to see your steps in present mode.
7. In **Present mode**, you will see that the frame you added to the path now fills the screen completely.

The frame that was added to the path fills the screen, as shown in the following screenshot:

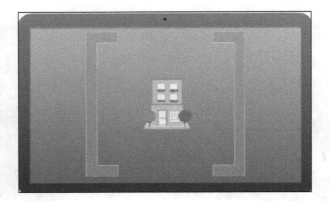

In the preceding screenshot, we created a step based on the frame. Thus, the frame fills the screen in **Present** mode.

 Frames are essential for zooming and tuning with Prezi. Learn more about the zoom effect in *Chapter 7, Zoom and Turn*.

Content in a frame

We obviously want great content in all our frames, and fortunately, this is easy to do. There are several ways to do it. Either way, adding content to a frame is a breeze!

You can either place a frame around an existing element, or you can create a frame and then add content to it.

How to do it...

1. Open the prezi that you want to work in.
2. Go to the **Frame** drop-down menu in the top-left corner and choose a frame type (any type of frame will work).
3. Click on the **+** sign or drag the frame icon to the right to insert the frame on the canvas.
4. Use the corner markers to adjust the frame's position and size to fit your needs.
5. Drag the frame over existing content or drag content into the frame.

Selecting multiple elements allows you to drag a multitude of elements into a frame.

There's more...

When a frame is created and initially put on the canvas, it is easy to adjust its size by pulling the corner markers. Once you have added content to the frame, adjusting the size of the frame will also impact the content.

To only adjust the frame, use this command to select the frame only: *Alt* + click to select. Now you have selected just the frame and are able to adjust its size without impacting the content. For a more detailed explanation, please refer to the *Editing a frame without impacting content* recipe in this chapter.

Removing content from a frame

As much as we try, very often we don't get things right the first time and we will have to edit the content on the canvas. And even if you carefully choose the elements that you put in your frame, there will be times when you will need to remove content from a frame, either to move it to someplace else or delete it entirely.

Removing content is no more difficult than adding it. All you have to do is select, drag, and drop the content.

How to do it...

1. Open the prezi that you want to work in.
2. Locate the frame that has the content you want to remove.
3. Click to select the element that you want to remove.
4. To delete it, press *Delete* on your keyboard.
5. To move it, drag the element out of the frame and drop it on the canvas or in another frame.

Use your mouse to select and drag an element out of a frame, as shown in the following screenshot:

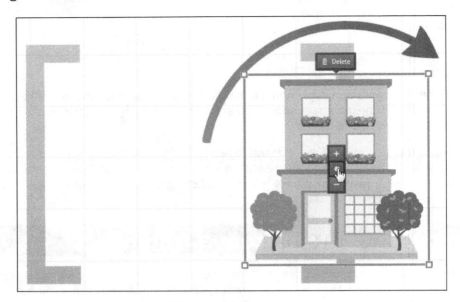

Selecting multiple elements allows you to drag a multitude of elements out of a frame in one operation. To select multiple elements, begin by holding down *Shift* and then click on the items you want to select.

Adjusting the size of a frame

For most of us, designing a prezi is a continuous process. One idea leads to the next, and along the way, we need to adjust our frames so that they match the content we finally decide to have in them. Fortunately, it is very easy to adjust the size of a frame.

Remember that when you select and edit your frame, you will also be editing the frame's content.

To learn how to adjust frames without impacting their content, please refer to the *Editing a frame without impacting content* recipe in this chapter.

How to do it...

1. Open the prezi that you want to work in.
2. Locate the frame that you want to resize.
3. Click on the visible part of the frame to select it.
4. To adjust to a larger size, pull the corner markers outwards.
5. To adjust to a smaller size, pull the corner markers inwards.

In the following screenshot, as we adjusted the size of our frame, the contents of the frame were equally impacted:

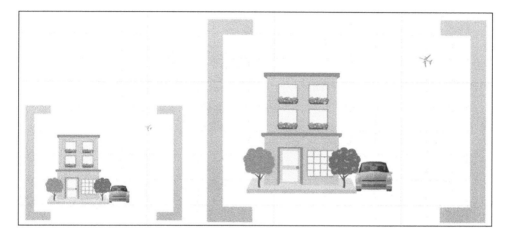

Turning a frame

As we develop our design and content, we will constantly be working on the placement of our frames. Turning a frame can add very interesting effects to your presentation, so this is a feature you will use a lot. In this recipe, we tell you how to apply a turn to a frame, and also how to adjust it. As you are about to see, it is the same process for both, and it is a very simple and straightforward process.

Remember that when you select and edit your frame, you will also be editing the frame's content. If you turn the frame, the elements inside will turn with the frame.

How to do it...

1. Open the prezi that you want to work in.

2. Locate the frame that you want to turn.

3. Click on the visible part of the frame to select it.

4. Hover over one of the corner markers to awaken the round marker.

5. Drag the round marker up or down to rotate the frame.

Rotate a frame by dragging the round marker (enlarged in the image), as shown in the following screenshot:

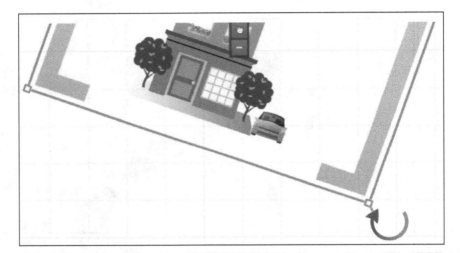

Moving a frame

A prezi is a work in progress, and edits are an inevitable part of the process. Planning ahead for your design will obviously save you some editing time, but even when we adhere to this principle, we will have to move frames around time and again. The good news is that it is very easy to move a frame.

Remember that when you select and edit your frame, you will also be editing the frame's content. So when you move a frame, the contents in the frame are moved with it.

How to do it...

1. Open the prezi that you want to work in.
2. Locate the frame that you want to move.
3. Click on the visible part of the frame to select it.
4. Drag the frame to a new position on the canvas.
5. Let go of the frame by dropping it in a new position.

 Any selected element on the Prezi canvas can be moved slightly by using the forward and backward arrows on the keyboard. This is very useful to fine-tune an element's placement.

Editing a frame without impacting content

While the auto setting for frames (and part of their purpose) is that whatever you do to your frame you are also doing to its content, there are ways to edit a frame without impacting the content.

There are two different ways: grabbing and dragging one side of frame or using the *Alt* key to select (only) the frame before editing. Both methods are worth memorizing because you will often need to adjust the size of a frame so that it better fits your purpose.

How to do it...

Method 1: Grab and drag one side of frame:

1. Open the prezi that you want to work in.
2. Locate the frame that you want to edit.
3. Make sure there is content in it.
4. Click on the visible part of the frame to select it.
5. Do not drag the corner handles (as this will impact the content).
6. Hover over any of the four blue lines until the double arrow is displayed.
7. Drag your preferred blue line to move it towards (or away from) the center of the frame.
8. Watch how your frame is now smaller (or bigger) while the frame's content is left unchanged.

Pull the thin blue line of a selected frame to adjust the height or width of the frame only. The bi-directional arrows are enlarged in the following screenshot for clarity:

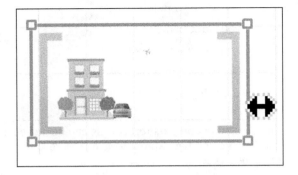

 Be aware that using this method to adjust the size of the frame will change its proportions. To change the size of a frame while maintaining frame proportions, use method 2.

Method 2: Select the frame using the *Alt* key:

1. Open the prezi that you want to work in.
2. Locate the frame that you want to edit.
3. Make sure there is content in it.
4. Hold down the *Alt* key.
5. While holding *Alt* key down, click on the frame to select it.
6. Drag the corner handles towards or away from the center to adjust the frame size.
7. Note that the change in the frame's size has not affected the content.
8. This method maintains the frame's proportions.

Hold down *Alt* and select the frame to adjust frame size proportionally, as shown in the following screenshot:

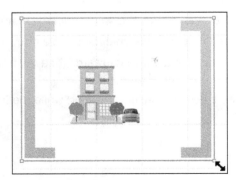

Be aware that using this method to adjust the size of the frame will maintain the frame's proportions.

To change a frame's proportions, use method 1.

The frame toolbar

All the frames in Prezi come with a small toolbar that is activated when the frame is selected. Take a look at the following screenshot:

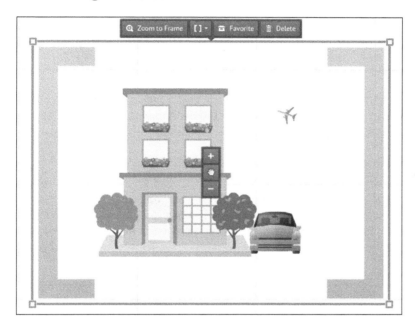

The Frame toolbar – Zoom to Frame

The **Zoom to Frame** option takes you exactly where you would expect it to. It zooms into the frame, thus allowing you easy access to edit the content. While this may sound simple, it is a very useful tool for presentations that use overlaid frames.

 This option does not allow you to edit the frame. It is intended to give you easy access to the contents of a specific frame.

The Frame toolbar – Replace or Delete frame

The **Frame** option is the icon in the middle of the toolbar. It provides a handy way to change the type of the selected frame. All you have to do is click to open the frame-picker menu, locate the frame you want, and then click on it. The options offered with **Frame** make it easy to switch frames or delete your frame without losing content:

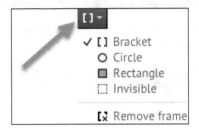

Another great characteristic for this command is that it allows you to delete your frame without deleting the content. Just go to the bottom of the list and click on **Remove frame**. Your frame will then be deleted, while your content will be preserved.

The Frame toolbar – Delete frame

Did you change your mind about a frame and now you need to get rid of it? Easy! The **Frame** toolbar's **Delete** option takes care of that for you. Mind you, this command deletes both the frame and its content. To delete the frame only, use *The Frame toolbar – Replace or Delete frame* recipe in this chapter. In the following screenshot, **Delete** on the toolbar removes the frame and its content:

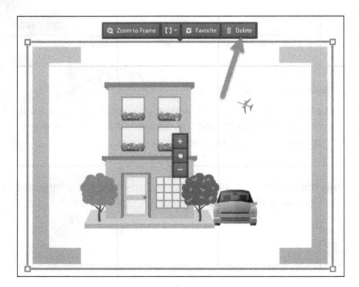

Deleting a frame – overview

There are several ways to delete a frame. Notice that some methods will also delete the content, while others allow you to keep the content even if the frame is deleted.

Getting ready

Select the frame you want to delete. Then use one of these methods:

Command	Result for content
The *Delete* key on the keyboard	This key will delete frame and content
The trash can icon on the frame toolbar	This icon will delete frame and content
The **Frame** option menu on frame toolbar	This option will delete frame, not content
Right-click on the frame, use menu	This action will delete frame, not content

Select the frame and right-click to access the right-click menu, as shown in the following screenshot:

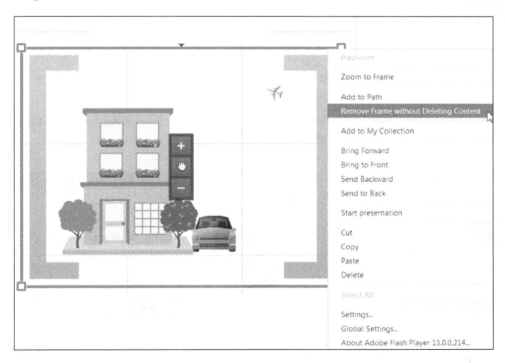

Prezi ratio

A prezi is designed to be viewed by your audience on a computer, via a projector, or on devices such as an iPad, iPhone, or Android. These output sources vary in their screen ratios. Most computer screens and monitors use the 16:9 format, whereas most projectors use 4:3.

Why do we need to know this? There are two reasons; a prezi looks better if its frames match the format of the output screen. Furthermore, the content of the individual frames presents itself better when it is designed specifically for the frame proportions that you will use when showing the prezi.

Some people think that this part of Prezi is a little hard to grasp. Actually, it's not that bad. Just read on and spend a little time studying the images carefully. You'll understand it all nice and easy.

Oh, and did we mention that it is easy to set the standard format for your frames? It is!

Prezi ratio and output source

Did you ever watch a movie on a TV screen that was set to wide screen even if the movie was not a wide screen movie? If so, you will know exactly why we need to fit our Prezi frames to the screen we will use to show the prezi; when content and output source match, things just look better!

So, if the ratios of the prezi and the output source don't match, will this prevent your prezi from running? Most certainly not; your prezi will run just fine.

However, take a close look at the following images to understand what happens when a 4:3 ratio prezi is shown on a 16:9 screen and vice versa:

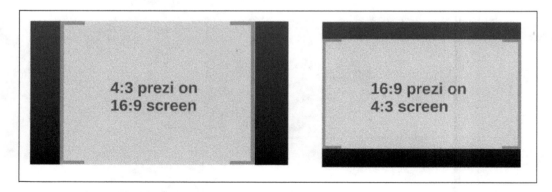

Prezis whose viewing ratio do not match the ratio of the output source will be shown with black bars around them to cover up the non-matching or excess part of the screen.

If you are anything like us, you'd rather not have the black bars around your prezi. That's why you want to set the right viewing ratio.

Prezi ratio and frames ratio

When you adjust the ratio for your prezi, you get a huge bonus. As of this moment, any rectangular frame that you create will automatically be created in the correct format to match your required ratio. The circle frames adjust automatically.

If you change the setting for your prezi at a point in time where you already have frames on the canvas, you will have to go back and manually edit each one of these frames to match the new format. It's likely that you will have to adjust the content as well to make it look nice.

For that reason, we highly recommend that you set the ratio for your frames before you do anything else in your prezi.

Whatever the output source for your prezi is, you want your prezi design, content, and frames to fit that source.

Remember that deciding your frame format is something you must consider for every individual prezi that you create, as the settings do not travel across your prezis.

The reason is that you will sometimes want to use the 16:9 format; at other times, you will want to use the 4:3 format. It all depends on what you are going to use your prezi for, and which device it will be viewed on.

Getting ready

Before you begin working on the canvas to create your prezi, find out how this prezi will most likely be viewed; will it be a 16:9 device or one whose proportions are 4:3?

How to do it...

This is how to choose and set the ratio for the prezi you are working in:

Open the prezi that you want to work in.

Go to the upper-right corner above the canvas and perform the following steps:

1. Click on the **Settings** menu (upper red arrow in the following image).
2. Click on **4:3** or **16:9** to set a standard ratio for this prezi (lower red arrow in the following image).
3. To close the menu (and save settings), just click on the canvas.

The following screenshot shows you where to set the frame ratio:

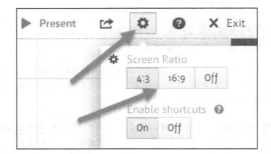

 Making sure that your prezi has the correct ratio setting before you begin working on the canvas saves you a lot of editing time later.

There's more...

Because Prezi cannot know which ratio settings you will need for each prezi, the default setting for ratio is **Off**.

If you do not actively choose either 4:3 or 16:9, you will not have set a ratio for your prezi.

This means that your prezi may not have a consistent look across various sizes (ratios) of output screens. So put yourself in control, by setting the ratio for your prezi.

 When the ratio setting is **Off**, your frames will be created in the 4:3 format but there will be no ratio set for the prezi to optimize the viewing experience.

As always, with prezi, it is easy to adjust the settings so that they fit your needs.

Frames troubleshooting

The following table lists a number of problems and their solutions:

Problem	Solution
Problem: "My prezi zooms to the correct frame but shows excess material." **Trigger**: Prezi zooms as close as possible to a frame. Here, the frame ratio does not fit the screen.	**Solution**: Adjust the frame ratio to fit the screen. Then redesign the frame content to fit the frame's new proportions (ratio).
Problem: "I want more space around this bracket frame." **Trigger**: Prezi zooms as close as possible to a frame.	**Solution**: Place an invisible frame (of a ratio that matches your set output ratio) around the bracket frame. Adjust its size to your liking and make this frame the step on the path.

Problem	Solution
Problem: "My prezi design looks different on my computer monitor than on a projector screen and when embedded on a website." **Trigger:** Your screen ratio has not been set, and Prezi cannot optimize the presentation to best fit the output screen ratio (by masking when necessary).	**Solution:** Choose a screen ratio in the **Settings** menu. Your prezi will now fit some screens perfectly and automatically be masked when it does not.
Problem: "I want my prezi to zoom and turn in on a detail." **Trigger:** Turn in a movement between two elements on the path happens only when these elements are placed on the canvas in different angles.	**Solution:** Turn the destination element (in this case, this is an invisible frame around the figure's head.) We turned the destination element by 90 degrees.

7
Zoom and Turn

In this chapter, we will cover the following recipes:

- ▶ Zoom in
- ▶ Zoom out
- ▶ Zooming with frames
- ▶ Zooming out with frames
- ▶ Zooming in with frames
- ▶ Turns
- ▶ Turning an element
- ▶ Turning a frame
- ▶ Anatomy of a turn
- ▶ Combining turns for elements and frames

Introduction

Many things about Prezi are distinctive, but two of the really special and characteristic features are the zoom and the turn.

A good way to understand zooming is to compare it with reading letters from your lawyer or your bank. When you switch from the general information to the small writing at the bottom of the page, you zoom in by moving the paper closer to your eyes. When you want to read the general information again, you zoom out by moving the paper further out.

The zoom feature allows us to zoom in on the canvas to show even the smallest detail, and to zoom out to show larger elements or beautiful and informative overviews.

Prezi's turning feature makes it possible for us to change the direction of our travel on the canvas as we move forward in the presentation.

In this chapter, we take a hands-on approach to the "how-to" of zooms and turns. When zooms and turns are used correctly, they become powerful tools that greatly enhance your prezi. We will show you how to create them, how you can combine them with each other, and how they apply to all the elements we can insert onto the canvas.

In *Appendix B, Transitions*, we will teach you how to use zooms and turns in a way that enhances your design and supports you as a presenter by helping your audience follow and understand your presentation.

See also

Zooming is easier to work with if you understand how to create and edit your prezi's path and steps. You can read about path and steps in *Chapter 5, Path and Steps*.

Zoom in

Zooming occurs between two steps in a prezi. Your work with zooms will be easier (and better) if you understand how steps work.

We invite you to follow along with this first recipe. It will quickly recap how steps work, and by following along, you will be able to create your first zoom.

 If you are unsure about steps but prefer skipping this recap, think of a step as either an element or a frame that you have decided to show when you are in the **Present** mode.

Getting ready

Because zooming happens between two steps, we begin by creating two steps. The content of these steps can be images, texts, frames, or any other element that has been added to the path. We will be working with images. Perform the following steps:

1. Open a new blank prezi.
2. Delete any existing frames.
3. Insert an image, sizing the image as you please. We inserted a red car.
4. Insert a second image. Make this image smaller than the first image. We inserted a green car.

Take a look at the following screenshot, where our prezi has two cars on the canvas; the green car is smaller than the red car:

How to do it...

Now you are just about ready to zoom:

1. Switch to the **Edit Path** mode.
2. First, click on the bigger image to add it as a step to the path lane.
3. Next, click on the smaller image to add it as a step to the path lane.
4. Click on **Present** to see how Prezi first shows step 1 and then zooms in to show step 2.

There! That was your first zoom. Pretty easy, eh?

We did it too! You can see it right here:

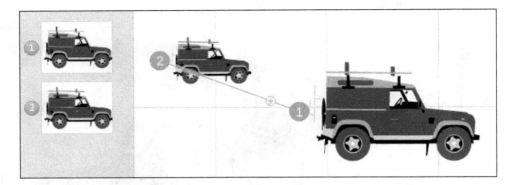

Both cars have been added as steps; steps are shown in the path lane as thumbnails.

There's more...

To understand the zoom, let's look at the preceding screenshot. Take a look at the two cars on the canvas and compare them to the thumbnails in the path lane. Remember that each thumbnail represents a step.

On the canvas there is a difference in the sizes of the two cars. But what is going on in the path lane? Here, in the path lane, the thumbnails for the red and the green cars show the cars at identical sizes. Hmmm! Does this mean that when we switch to the **Present** mode, Prezi will show the two cars at the same size?

Yes, that is exactly what it means! What a thumbnail shows is exactly how the step that it represents will be shown in the **Present** mode.

For this prezi, it means that when we click on **Present**, the red car will fill the screen entirely. When we move forward to step 2, the green car will also fill the screen entirely.

This is how steps function: a step always fills the screen.

And that is the anatomy of the zoom! Zooming happens because a step always fills the screen in **Present** mode. Consequently, if two steps have different sizes on the canvas, Prezi needs to zoom in or out to allow whatever step is next to fill the screen.

 Remember the equation for steps: *1 step = 1 full screen*

Zoom out

Zooming out means going from a smaller section of the canvas to a relatively bigger section of the canvas in the **Present** mode.

Zooming out is a great tool that is typically used for visual illustrations on the canvas, when the content of the presentation shifts from a detailed level to some degree of overview of the canvas.

The biggest zoom-outs in Prezi are path steps that are overviews of the entire canvas, which many presenters use to open or close their presentations.

Getting ready

1. Open a new blank prezi.
2. Delete any existing frames.
3. Insert an image, sizing it as you please. We inserted a green car.
4. Insert a second image. Make this image larger than the first image. We inserted a red car.

We will use the prezi shown in the following screenshot. We want our presentation to begin by showing the green car. Then we want it to zoom out so that the next step shows the red car.

How to do it...

1. Switch to the **Edit Path** mode.
2. First, click on the smaller image to add it as a step to the path lane.
3. Then, select the larger image to add it as a step to the path lane.
4. Click on **Present** to see how Prezi first shows step 1 and then zooms out to show the bigger step 2.

Take a look at the following screenshot, where both cars have been added as steps; steps are shown in the path lane as thumbnails:

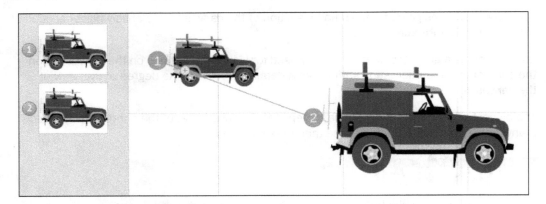

Zooming with frames

When we work in Prezi, we often need to zoom in or out to show a section or specific area of the canvas, rather than a single element. Sometimes the section that we want to show is small; sometimes it is a larger section.

This is easily done with frames. Frames are a fantastic tool because they put you in the driver's seat. By carefully using frames, it is possible to target the exact area of the canvas that we want to show.

In the following text and recipes, we will be using a red bracket frame for most purposes. That is because we want to ensure that the frame is clearly visible to you.

Normally in Prezi, the reality about zooms is that we typically use invisible frames. Invisible frames are our favorite for zooming purposes because they do not interfere with style, colors, or the general design of our prezi.

Take a look at the following screenshot, where the invisible frames on the car to the right do not disturb the design:

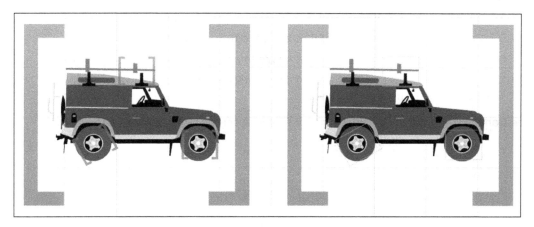

See also

► Read *Chapter 6, Frames and Prezi Ratio,* if you want to recollect how to choose and insert frames.

Zooming out with frames

It is easy to zoom out to any section on the canvas using frames. All you have to do is frame the section that you want to show. Then set that frame as a step, and you are ready to go to that frame in the **Present** mode, where Prezi will show the chosen (framed) section of the canvas.

Getting ready

Perform the following steps on a new prezi:

1. Open a new blank prezi.
2. Delete any existing frames.
3. Insert an image, sizing it as you please.

How to do it...

1. In the top-left corner, choose a frame type in the **Frame** drop-down menu (you may use any type).
2. Click on the frame icon to insert the frame into the canvas.
3. Insert and adjust the frame so that it encloses the image and leaves a nice amount of space around it.

4. Switch to the **Edit Path** mode.

5. First, select the image to add it as a step to the path lane.

6. Then select the frame around the image to add it as step 2 to the path lane.

7. Click on **Present** to see how Prezi shows step 1 (the image) and then zooms out to step 2 (the frame).

The frame around the car, as shown in the following screenshot, enables us to zoom out:

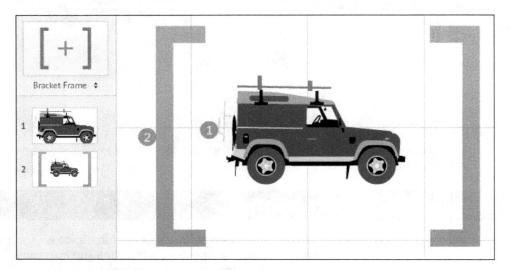

There's more...

Overviews are used a lot in most Prezi presentations. The overview can be of a portion of the information on the canvas, such as a chapter overview, or it can include your entire Prezi. Overviews are great because they help your audience get just that—an overview!

It is easy to create an overview. Just frame the section of the canvas that you want to show, add it to the path, and that's it!

The following is a screenshot showing an overview of all the images we have used so far in this chapter:

Zooming in with frames

It is easy to zoom in or out to any section on the canvas using frames. Just frame the section that you want to show and set that frame as a step.

This recipe demonstrates how to zoom in. We will be zooming into a detail of a car, but you can use these steps to perform any movement from a larger section to a smaller section on the canvas.

Getting ready

Perform the following steps on a new prezi:

1. Open a new blank prezi.
2. Insert an image.
3. Delete any existing frames.

How to do it...

1. In the top-left corner, choose a frame type in the **Frame** drop-down menu (you may use any type).
2. Click on the frame icon to insert the frame on the canvas.
3. Drag the frame onto a detail of the image.
4. Resize the frame to your liking by pulling any of the four corner markers of the frame.

5. Switch to the **Edit Path** mode.

6. Now select the image to add it as a step to the path lane.

7. Then select your new frame to add it as step 2 to the path lane.

8. Click on **Present** to see how Prezi shows step 1 (the full image) and then zooms in to show step 2 (the frame).

Take a look at the following screenshot, where the full image of the car is step 1 and the frame is step 2:

When you click on **Present**, the prezi will show the car (step 1) and then zoom in to show the frame (step 2), allowing you to see the wheel closely.

Turns

Prezi allows us to create turning effects.

The turn feature makes it possible to change directions as we move forward in the presentation.

Turns have the potential of adding great dynamics to your Prezi presentation. If used correctly, turns can be a powerful tool that actively support your message.

The following recipes will show you how to easily create turns for elements and frames. Towards the end of the chapter, we will also show you how combining frames and turns create interesting effects.

In *Appendix B, Transitions*, we will show you how to integrate zooms and turns with your overall design.

How it works...

When you place an element on the canvas, it is not turned. It is in its original or "right-way-up" position.

Now suppose you switch to **Present** mode, and begin moving forward through the steps in your presentation. When a step is shown, the element that is that is this step will always be shown at its original (right-way-up) position, no matter how much you turned it on the canvas.

So, if the elements actually do not turn, how does Prezi create this turning effect? Well, as we are about to see, it is actually the canvas that is being turned. Read on!

There's more...

When we refer to elements that can be turned, it is important to keep in mind that this can be any element that you can put on the canvas. Images, videos, PDF files, text elements, and frames are all elements that can be turned.

Confused? Don't be! Try it out on your canvas. It's pretty easy, and you'll quickly get the hang of it.

[

Frame troubles? You may want to check out the *Frames troubleshooting* section of *Chapter 6, Frames and Prezi Ratio*.
]

Turning an element

Turns create a feel of action that is great for grabbing the attention of your audience. Fortunately, you can easily turn any selected element on the canvas. For this recipe, we will be using an image.

Getting ready

Perform the following steps on a new prezi:

1. Open a new blank prezi.
2. Delete any existing frames.
3. Insert an image.
4. Notice how the image looks on the canvas in its right-way-up position.

How to do it...

1. Click on the image to select it.
2. Hover over any one of the square-shaped corner markers.
3. This activates the turning tool (the circle handle).
4. Grab the turning tool and drag it up or down to turn the image.
5. Place the image in its final position by releasing your mouse key.

The turning handle is shown in the following screenshot. Use it to drag up or down to turn the selected element:

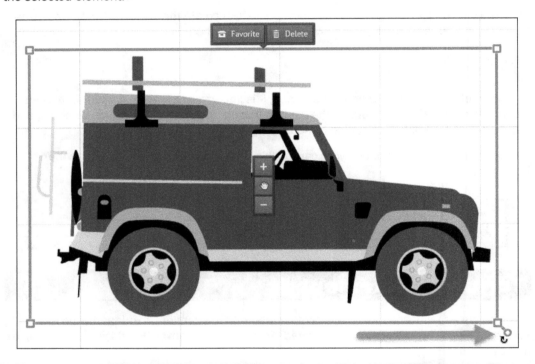

Turning a frame

Any element on the canvas can be turned. This applies to frames as well. Practice by experimenting, and you will gradually develop a good sense of how turned frames work on the canvas.

Getting ready

Perform the following steps on a new prezi:

1. Open a new blank prezi.
2. Insert any frame (except the circle frame, which makes it difficult to notice the turn).

How to do it...

1. Click on the frame to select it.
2. Hover over any one of the square-shaped corner markers.
3. This activates the turning tool (the circle handle).
4. Grab the turning tool and drag it up or down to turn the frame.
5. Place it in its chosen final position by releasing your mouse button.

In the following screenshot, use the turning handle to drag up or down to turn the frame:

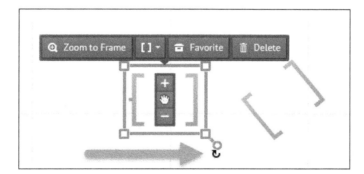

Anatomy of a turn

The following image provides an overview of the zooms and turns we discussed in this chapter:

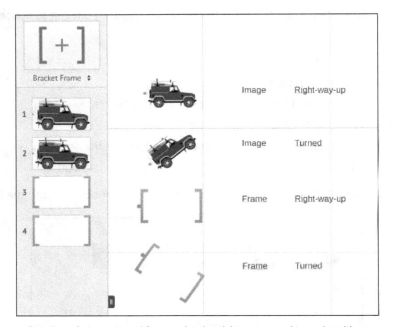

Overview of elements and frames showing right-way-up and turned positions

To study the anatomy of turns, let's take a look at the preceding screenshot:

Step	Element	Canvas	Path lane (and present mode)
1	Image	Right-way-up image	▸ Image is shown right way up ▸ Image fills the screen
2	Image	Turned image	▸ Image is shown right way up ▸ Canvas must turn ▸ Image fills the screen
3	Frame	Right-way-up frame	▸ Frame is shown right way up ▸ Frame fills the screen
4	Frame	Turned frame	▸ Frame is shown right way up ▸ Canvas must turn ▸ Frame fills the screen

There's more...

If you need to edit a frame without affecting the content, you can do so by selecting only the frame. This is done by holding down the *Alt* key while using you mouse to select the frame. Once the frame is selected, you can edit its size and position (including turning) as it pleases you.

For more keyboard shortcuts, please refer to *Appendix C, Keyboard Shortcuts*.

[Did you notice that other elements sometimes get highlighted when you turn an element? This reflects that their angle is similar to the element you are editing.]

Combining turns for elements and frames

Take a look at the following screenshot, where turned elements that are steps make the canvas turn when in **Present** mode:

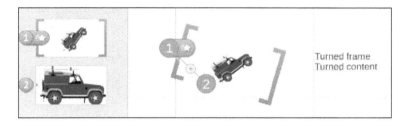

Turned frame
Turned content

Step	Element	Canvas	Path lane (and present mode)
1	Frame	Frame is turned	► Frame is shown right way up ► Canvas must turn ► Frame fills the screen
2	Image	Image is turned	► Image is shown right way up ► Canvas must turn ► Image fills the screen

[Zooms and turns can be combined in numerous ways, and the best way to get the feel of them is by experimenting on the canvas. Go for it!]

8

Animation

In this chapter, we will cover the following recipes:

- ▶ How animated elements are activated for presentation
- ▶ Before you animate
- ▶ Animation tools
- ▶ Animating elements
- ▶ Resetting or deleting animation
- ▶ Line-by-line fade-in of text
- ▶ Animating grouped elements

Introduction

All the keywords, images, videos, and other material in your prezi are there because you want the audience to see it, and because the audience will be interested. It is likely that everything on the canvas will be carefully studied by them to be fully enjoyed and understood.

The thing is that this process takes a little time. And during this time, because the audience is focusing on the visuals, they will not be able to fully focus on you or anything you might say.

Once you know this, it is easy to handle. All you have to do is plan for it. The basic idea is to plan so that you do not deliver two messages (visual and verbal) at the same time.

For everything you say, show just the visuals that accompany that information—and only those visuals. Then, when you need to show something more, allow the audience a few seconds to take it in.

Prezi offers a tool that helps you do this. This tool is called animation.

Animation allows us to hide any element (text, pictures, or other elements) until we want it to appear. It will fade in when activated by a mouse click.

The primary use of the animation feature in Prezi is to give the audience just the right dose of information at a time. Animation is a way of helping your audience better understand your message. It may, of course, also serve as a cool and fun effect that you can use to surprise your audience.

In this chapter, we will teach you how to make animations. We show you how to create them and how you can edit and reset your animations. We will also show you how to fade-in a group of elements.

Fade-in is the only available animation option in Prezi.

See also

To apply animation of your content, your prezi must be in the **Edit Path** mode. You will also need the content that you want to animate in frames. You can read about frames in *Chapter 6, Frames and Prezi Ratio*, and learn more about editing paths in *Chapter 5, Path and Steps*.

How are animated elements activated for presentation?

To make animated elements appear, switch to present mode and then just click on the forward command (mouse click, play arrows on the screen, or others) as you always do for presenting. The animated elements will appear as you move forward through your steps. Take a look at the following screenshot:

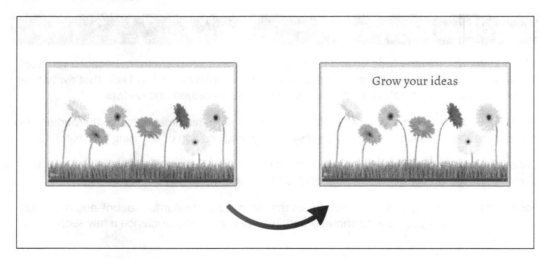

The fade-in effect is activated only in present mode. When in present mode, animated elements appear as you move forward in your presentation, working your way through frames and animations on your path.

 When you are in edit mode, all animated elements are visible on the canvas. Animated elements can be edited in the same way as any other element.

Examples of animated elements

In the following bullets, we have listed some elements that we use the animation feature for:

- ▶ **Bullets**: Reveal bullets one point at a time
- ▶ **Diagram**: Show parts of a flow diagram as you introduce them
- ▶ **Large image**: Zoom in on the details and reveal extra information
- ▶ **Surprise**: Hide some parts of an overall picture to reveal it later

As you work with Prezi and gain experience in applying animation, you will develop other uses for it. Be creative and have fun!

 The wow factor that comes from using animations in prezis is likely to be diminished if too many animations are used. Make sure you don't over saturate your prezi with them.

Before you animate

Whenever you animate and whatever the element that you want to animate, the underlying prerequisites and the workflow are the same. If you understand the prerequisites, working with animation will be easy. Ready? Here we go!

Frame elements

Any element that you want to animate must be in a frame. This is a "no exception" rule. It does not matter which kind of frame you choose. Any kind of frame will work, so the choice of frame is merely cosmetic. These are Prezi's frames:

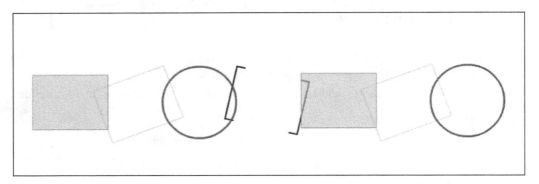

However, what does matter is whether your element (or elements) is completely inside your chosen frame. There are no exceptions to this rule, and even the tiniest bit of an element outside a frame will prevent you from applying animation to that element.

There's more...

The frame also needs to be on the path. Think about this:

- ▶ Animated elements are meant to appear when in present mode
- ▶ The elements that you want to show in present mode are what you add to the path

Seen that way, it makes very good sense that you cannot animate something in a frame if this frame is not on the path.

 Make sure your text elements do not have textboxes that are much longer than the actual text. When closed, the length of a textbox is invisible and may easily be outside the frame, which is not acceptable for animation.

Animation tools

We use animation in Prezi to temporarily withhold information, to create a surprise effect, or just for beautification and a wow effect.

Elements that you want to animate need to be in a frame. This frame needs to be added to the path. It all happens in **Edit Path** mode. Let's find out how!

Take a look at the following screenshot, where frames on the path have a star next to their number; this is visible only in the **Edit Path** mode:

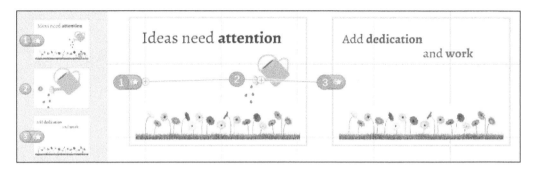

Animation stars

Our prezi, as shown in the preceding screenshot, is now in the **Edit Path** mode.

Looking at the blue, numbered circles in the path lane and on the canvas, we notice that some of these have a small star next to them, while others don't.

The stars are animation stars. They are Prezi's way of telling you that a step can be animated. Our steps 1 and 2 both have the star, so they can be animated. If a step has no star (such as step 3), it cannot be animated.

The reason for the difference is that steps 1 and 3 are frames. Any content in them can be animated. Step 2 is an unframed element, and therefore, it cannot be animated (remember, elements must be in a frame to be animated).

Animation dialogue box

To create an animation, you need to use the animation dialogue box.

The animation dialogue box is easily recognized by its black bar with **Animation** written in white. This box is your gateway to creating and editing your animations.

As previously mentioned and shown in the preceding screenshot, steps that can be animated have a star next to them in the **Edit Path** mode. Click on the star for a frame to open the **Animation** dialogue box for that frame. Take a look at the **Animation** dialogue box shown in the following screenshot:

 Clicking on one of the available animation stars is the only way to open and access the animation dialogue box.

Now you are ready to begin animating. Just follow the next recipe.

Animating elements

Fade-in animation is easy and fun to work with and with a few rounds of practice you'll get it just right. So let's get started! Please join us when we take a look at the recipe below.

Getting ready...

1. Open your prezi.
2. Arrange the elements you want to animate in a frame.
3. Ensure that all the elements are completely inside the frame.
4. Ensure that the frame is added to the path.

How to do it...

1. Switch to **Edit Path** mode.
2. Click on the animation star for the frame you want to work with (choose the star on the canvas or in the path). Now the **Animation** dialogue box opens.
3. First, click on the element you want to fade in as number one. A green star appears, showing the number one, indicating that this is the first element to fade in.
4. Click on any additional elements that you want to animate. Additional green stars with numbers indicating the order in which elements fade in will appear.
5. Close the window by clicking on **Done**.

Take a look at the following screenshot:

Animations are meant to be shown in **Present** mode and will be visible there. Animations are not active on the canvas in edit mode. To watch or check your animation, switch to present mode or reopen the animation dialogue box.

There's more...

In the process of working in the **Animation** dialogue box to add animation to our elements, it is often helpful to perform a test run of the animations. A test run helps you check whether you've animated all the elements that you planned to, and that they fade in in the correct order.

Prezi provides a play button for this. It is located in the animation dialogue box in the top-right corner. Use it to run a test drive of your animations without having to exit the **Animation** dialogue box.

As shown in the following screenshot, click on the play button in the animation dialogue box to view your animation:

 Click on **Present** to view the animation in present mode as well. Sometimes, you will find that your animations have a different visual effect when viewed in full screen.

Resetting or deleting animation

No matter how carefully we plan and create our animations, we will sometimes need to go back to adjust or maybe even completely cancel an entire animation. Fortunately, editing an animation sequence is super easy!

Getting ready

1. Open your prezi.

2. Identify the frame that holds the animations you want to edit (if you have a lot of frames on your canvas, this sometimes requires a little investigation).

> The fastest way to zoom into a frame is to click on the frame in the path lane. Another good method is to click on it on the canvas and choose **Zoom to frame**.

How to do it...

1. Switch to the **Edit Path** mode.

2. Click on the animation star for the frame with the animated content that you want to edit. This opens the animation dialogue box.

3. To reset (cancel) all animations in this frame, click on **Reset** in the top-left corner of the animation dialogue box.

4. To reset (cancel) animation for a single animated element, hover over its green star and then click on the emerging red circle with **X** in it.

5. Close the animation dialogue box by clicking on **Done**.

Take a look at the following screenshot:

To cancel all animations for this frame, use the **Reset** button. To cancel a single animation, hover your mouse over a green star to produce the red **X** circle.

Line-by-line fade-in of text

One of the reasons that we love animation is that we can use it to control at what time a specific image or other piece of information will be revealed.

Often, you will have a list of subjects on your canvas that you would want to talk about one by one. In such cases, you may want to reveal one element at a time to help your audience focus on one subject at a time.

In this recipe, you can see how easy it is to set up animations so that listed text elements fade in one by one.

Getting ready

Creating a list in which bullets or subjects can be animated to appear one by one requires each bullet or subject on the list to be a separate text element.

Prezi's built in bulleted list creates bullets that are separate elements that share a textbox. However, as long as they are in the same textbox, you cannot animate the bullets individually. To create separate textboxes, drag each bullet out of the original textbox and re-arrange the bullets to your liking (in a frame).

Now perform the following steps:

1. Ensure that all text elements in your list are separate text elements.
2. Ensure that all text elements are in the frame you are using and that all text elements are completely within that frame.

How to do it...

1. Switch to the **Edit Path** mode.
2. Click on the animation star for the frame that holds the content you want to animate. This opens the **Animation** dialogue box.
3. Click on the first text element you want to fade in. A green star appears with the number 1 in it, indicating that this is the first element to fade in.
4. Continue to click on the elements in the order in which you want them to appear.
5. Use the **Play** button (top-right corner) to check whether you've got the sequence right.
6. Close the **Animation** dialogue box by clicking on **Done**.

Now, take a look at the following screenshot:

Make the months appear one by one by creating a separate textbox and animation for each.

 Note that a bulleted list created with Prezi's bullet feature can only be animated after you have separated the bullets so that they all are single-text elements.

See also

▸ Refer to *Chapter 2, Inserting Text, Images, and Links*.

Animating grouped elements

As you continue to work in Prezi and gain more and more experience, you may want to do something with your animations that is a little more advanced than just animating single elements. You may want to add animation to a group of elements.

Animating a group of elements is a way to reveal any portion of your content on the screen when you want it to be visible. You may want to use it for a complete section of your prezi, or for an element on a list to emerge at the same time as a related graphic element. Or maybe you have combined a number of graphic elements and want these to appear as one beautiful graphic element.

Animating groups is a highly useful feature that you will eventually use a lot. So let's get started!

Getting ready

The key concept is to group the elements that you want to appear together. Once the elements are grouped, Prezi considers the group to be one element, and you can animate it as you would animate any other element. Now perform the following steps:

1. Open your prezi.
2. Group the elements you want to appear (animate) together
3. If you want multiple groups in the same frame, choose and group elements for each group.

 You can group elements by selecting your chosen elements and clicking on **Group** in the toolbar above the selected elements.

You can read more about grouping elements in *Chapter 4, Editing Elements on the Canvas*.

How to do it...

1. Switch to **Edit Path** mode.

2. Click on the animation star for the frame that holds the content you want to animate. This opens the **Animation** dialogue box.

3. Click on the first group you want to fade in. A green star appears with the number 1 in it, indicating that this is the first group to fade in.

4. Continue clicking on groups and other elements in the order in which you want them to appear.

5. Use the play button (the triangle at the top-right corner) to check whether you've got the sequence right.

6. Close the **Animation** dialogue box by clicking on **Done**.

Now, take a look at the following screenshot, where we've grouped a few social media icons and two text elements:

There's more...

If you need to edit a grouped element that you have animated, you must ungroup it to edit or rearrange your elements. You must then regroup and reapply the animation.

The only exception from this rule is for text elements. A text element can be edited individually, even if it is part of a group.

To edit a text element, double-click on the text to activate its edit mode.

To move a text element onto the canvas, grab the upper grey part of the textbox and drag it to a new position.

 As your prezis become more advanced and you nest layers of grouped elements and frames, ungrouping and reapplying animations can be quite time-consuming. You can save time by finishing your prezi before you start adding animation.

9
Reuse Favorite Frames and Elements

In this chapter, we will cover the following recipes:

- ▶ Saving favorites to My Content
- ▶ Inserting items from My Content
- ▶ Reusing Prezi template elements via My Content
- ▶ Copying elements from one prezi to another
- ▶ Inserting layouts
- ▶ Customizing layouts
- ▶ Inserting tables and graphs created in Word and Excel

Introduction

When you have worked in Prezi for some time and understand the fundamental principles and commands of Prezi, it is likely that you will begin to want to perform more advanced actions.

In this chapter, we will show you how to take advantage of some Prezi's advanced features. Knowing how to transfer and reuse great elements or whole sections between the prezis in your Prezi account enables you to reuse material so that you will not have to spend time recreating what you already created once.

If you ever wondered how to transfer elements between your prezis, how to work with diagrams, or if it is possible to integrate Prezi with other programs, this is the chapter for you.

The feature that we use for this is **My Content.** This is your personal library where you can store your favorite material, such as images, diagrams, and even complete presentations. Storing your favorite material here saves you time because it is often quicker to rework or alter an existing design than to create an element from scratch.

We will show you how to insert and edit Prezi's own diagrams, and top it all off by teaching you to integrate (reuse) material from other programs, such as Word and Excel.

The know-how of this chapter will help you create prezis that stand out from other presentations by being more exciting.

See also

To read about how you can reuse material from your favorite PowerPoint presentations, please refer to *Chapter 14, PowerPoint and Prezi.*

My Content – your collection of favorites

Sometimes the material used in a prezi is so beautiful or useful that you will wish to reuse it in one or more future presentations.

You may have an illustration that would be useful for many Prezi purposes, or you may have spent a lot of time developing a Prezi diagram for your marketing department, only to realize that this diagram is relevant for other departments and prezis as well.

To do this, you use **My Content. My Content** is your collection of favorite elements, much like a library or treasure chest.

My Content is very easy to use. All you have to do is designate an element as a favorite. That an element is a favorite means that it has been added to the **My Content** collection.

Your collection of favorites (**My Contents**) belongs to the prezi account in which the elements were named favorites. If you have more than one Prezi account, you will have multiple collections—one for each account.

The collection of favorites (**My Contents**) from one account cannot be accessed from other accounts.

 To transfer elements or content from one Prezi account to another, use different browsers and *Ctrl + C* and *Ctrl + V* to copy and paste (or read further).

Saving favorites to My Content

My Content is your collection of favorite elements. A favorite element can be anything that is on the Prezi canvas. Examples range from texts to beautiful graphics and even entire presentations.

It is easy to save any selected element(s) to **My Contents**, and it is just as easy to access the collection to insert some of the good stuff on the canvas.

[Open the **Insert** menu to access your favorites in **My Content**. Learn how in the *Inserting items from My Content* recipe in this chapter.]

Getting ready

Now, perform the following steps:

1. Open your prezi.
2. Zoom out to show the element(s) you want to add to **My Content**.

How to do it...

1. Click to select the element you want to add to **My Content**.
2. To insert multiple elements, select these elements by pressing *Shift* and clicking on the elements one by one.
3. A thin line frames the selected elements. On top of the frame, the small toolbar displays **Favorite**.
4. Click on **Favorite** on this toolbar and watch how your selected element(s) travels across the canvas towards the **Insert** menu.

As shown in the following screenshot, select your element(s) and choose **Favorite** to add elements to **My Content**:

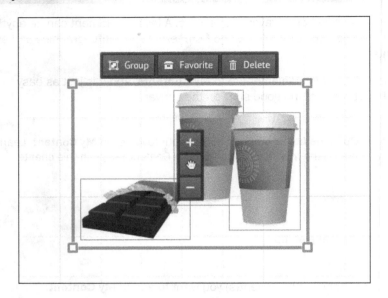

 Another way to save elements to **My Content** is to right-click on a selected element. In the right-click menu, you will find the **Add to Favorites** menu option.

Make it a habit to add images and designs that you like to **My Content**. This way you will always have great material to insert in your prezis, even if you are pressed for time.

There's more...

We often get the question, "What is the maximum size for an element that you want to store in **My Content**?". To be honest, we don't have the answer. The simple reason is that we have not yet found any limits.

The fact is that it is possible to store huge amounts of material in **My Content**. It is even possible to select and store the content of an entire prezi, should you choose to do so.

Inserting items from My Content

My Content is your personal library where you can store your favorite material.

My Content has two sections. In the first section, you have access to items previously stored as **Favorites**. This can be images, diagrams, or perhaps the full presentation to reuse in other prezis. In the other section, you have access to frames from all prezis that you previously created.

Reusing good material is a great option because it saves you from recreating similar items over and over again. Even if you need the item slightly altered, it is often quicker to rework or alter an existing design than to create an element from scratch.

Inserting favorites from My Content

Reusing good material is a great option because it saves you from recreating similar items over and over again. Even if you need the item slightly altered, it is often quicker to rework or alter an existing design than to create an element from scratch.

Getting ready

Now, perform the following steps:

1. Open your prezi.
2. Zoom in on the section of your prezi in which you want to insert content.

How to do it...

1. Click on **Insert**.
2. Choose **My Content**. Click on **Favorites**.
3. This opens the content menu on the right side of your canvas.
4. Point, click, and hold to drag any one of the thumbnails to the canvas.

Take a look at the following screenshot, where the **My Content** window to the right of the canvas shows the material in this account's content library:

Inserting favorite frames with My Content

Some of the frames that you create in a prezi are so great that it would be good to reuse them in other prezis. **My Content** helps you do that as well. **My Content** offers direct access to all the prezis you previously created.

It is important to remember that only frames that are on a path in a prezi will be shown here.

Getting ready

Now, perform the following steps:

1. Open a new prezi.
2. Open a prezi you previously created (to make sure you have at least one other prezi to transfer frames from).

How to do it...

1. Click on **Insert**.
2. Choose **My Content**.
3. Click on **From Prezis** in the content menu on the right side of your canvas.
4. Scroll down to locate the desired prezi.
5. Click on **See all** to access all the available frames from this prezi.
6. Decide which frame (thumbnail) you want to use.
7. Click and drag the desired thumbnail onto the canvas.

Take a look at the following screenshot, where in **My Content** you choose **From Prezis** to access frames from all the prezis in your account:

Navigating to **My Content** | **From Prezis** has a nifty search function. Use it to search for any word in a prezi; it doesn't matter whether the word is found in the title or text within the prezi. The search bar is located just above the prezi thumbnails.

Reusing Prezi template elements via My Content

Many Prezi templates contain beautiful and useful graphic elements that can easily be saved to **My Content**. Saving these graphics for reuse is a great way to begin building your collection of favorites.

You can use **My Content** to save a design template as a complete design that you can reuse. Alternatively, you may choose to save and reuse only select graphic elements from a template.

Both choices provide easy access to great graphic material to get your collection started.

Getting ready

Now, perform the following steps:

1. Access your Prezi account.
2. Choose **New Prezi**.
3. Choose a template and click on **Use template**.

For this example, we used a template called *Take the Plunge* for our new prezi.

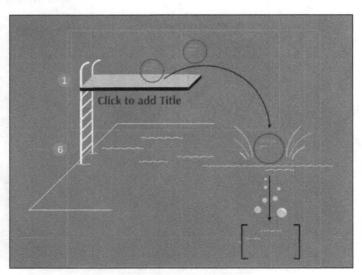

Now you need to decide whether you want to save all the elements in this template or you would rather pick one or a few. We will show you both—read on!

How to do it...

To add the entire content (frames, text elements, and graphic elements) from this template to **My Content**, you must:

1. Create a selection that includes all elements on the canvas.
2. On the toolbar above the selected elements, choose **Favorite**.

Take a look at the following screenshot, where we selected the encompassing invisible frame and can now add it to **My Content**:

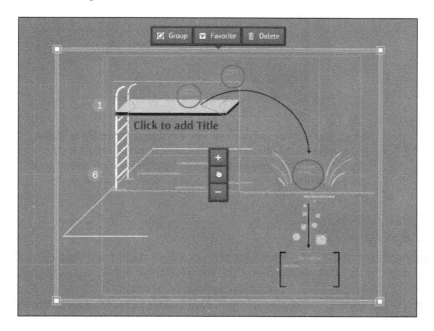

To add a single element from a template to **My Content**, most times you will need to begin by ungrouping the material in the template. This is easy to do!

1. Select the group that holds the element(s) that you want to save.
2. On the toolbar above the selected elements, click on **Ungroup** (note that some graphics may be integrated in the background and not eligible for ungrouping).

3. Now select a single element or multiple elements by clicking on the element.

4. When the element is selected, use the toolbar above the element or right-click pop-up menu to add the selected element to **Favorites**.

As shown in the following screenshot, click on **Ungroup** to access single elements in a group:

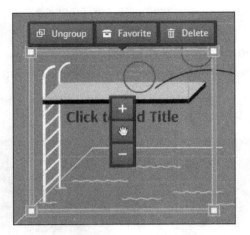

 When you select multiple elements to add them to **My Content**, it's entirely up to you whether you want to group these. If you do, they will be added as a group; if not, they will be added as a multi-unit favorite.

There's more...

Some of the elements in the Prezi templates have colors that are controlled by the underlying color theme of the prezi. This means that if you insert such an element on the canvas, it will potentially look different in various prezis, depending on which color theme you chose for the prezi into which you want to insert this element. Now take a look at the following screenshot:

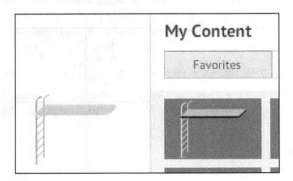

Compare the two diving boards in the preceding screenshot. The board and ladder are made by Prezi lines and shapes. The one in the **Favorites** collection to the right is the original diving board that we copied from the *Take the Plunge* template.

To the left in the picture is what the diving board looks like when inserted into a prezi that is based on the blank template.

 Prezi's collection of templates is constantly updated. New templates are added, other templates are removed. If a template has elements that you like, save these today rather than tomorrow. This way you will always have access to this material.

Copying elements from one prezi to another

My Content is a great functionality to store favorite elements for reuse in other prezis. However, sometimes all you need is to quickly copy an element from one prezi to another without wanting to store the element for repeated use, or maybe you are pressed for time, and don't want to spend time looking for a particular frame via **My Content | From Prezis**.

When all you need is to quickly copy an element from one prezi to another, a good old fashioned copy and paste process is a faster and simple way to go.

All you have to do is keep two prezis open at the same time, and just copy elements from one prezi to another.

This is the quickest way to reuse or transfer an element from one prezi to another.

Getting ready

Now, perform the following steps:

1. Open the prezi that you want to insert content into.
2. In the browser window, go to the tab called **Your Prezis**.
3. Locate and open a second prezi from which you will copy elements.

How to do it...

1. In the second prezi (the one you want to copy from), right-click on the element you want to copy.
2. In the right-click menu, choose **Copy**.
3. Go to the first prezi (by clicking its tab in the browser window).

4. Right-click on the canvas where you want to insert the element.

5. In the right-click menu, choose **Insert**.

 Some Prezi elements have colors that are controlled by the underlying template of the prezi. Be aware that these elements might change color when inserted in a Prezi that uses a different template. The image of the diving boards on the previous page is a good example of this.

Now take a look at the following screenshot, where right-clicking on selected element(s) displays a pop-up menu that gives you access to copying:

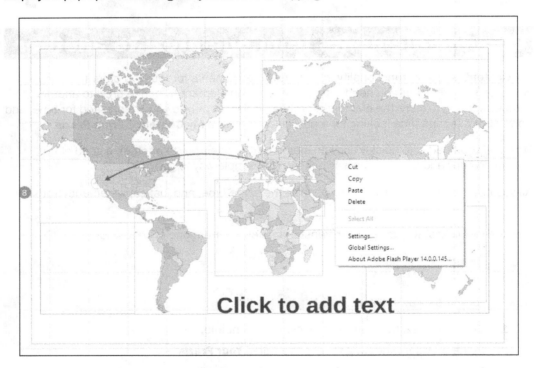

 The preceding map is copied from one of the Prezi templates. Many Prezi templates contain great graphics that you can easily copy for your own prezi.

There's more...

Copying material from one prezi to another works well even if you work in different Prezi accounts at the same time.

See also

If you want to insert several elements at once and are uncertain how to create groups, please refer to *Chapter 4, Editing Elements on the Canvas.*

If you prefer, Prezi's keyboard shortcuts contain the same functions for copying, inserting, and much more. Please refer to the overview of Prezi's shortcut keys at the back of this book.

Layouts

Layouts in Prezi are a collection of ready-made elements that are designed to help you work faster and smarter by offering easy access to placeholders. Placeholders are pre-designed elements that will hold either text or a picture.

Layouts are found in the **Insert** menu, as shown in the following screenshot:

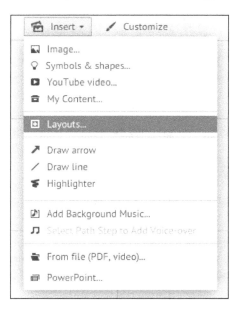

Layouts include two categories; one category holds single-frame objects and the other holds multi-frame objects, as shown in the following screenshot:

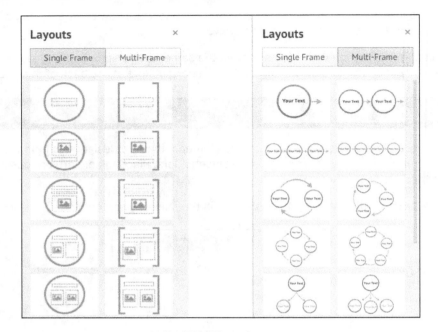

Any layout that you like is easily inserted onto the canvas just by dragging with your mouse.

How it works...

The **Layouts** in Prezi are a collection of Prezi frames that hold placeholders for text and images.

The placeholders are frames and text elements, pre-made for your content. The types of frames that are offered include circle and bracket frames. The number and character of the placeholders within the frames vary.

There are two categories of layouts; single-frame layouts with just a single frame, and multi-frame layouts that contain multiple frames connected by arrows and lines.

Layouts offer a quick way to create and add content to frames on the canvas.

Inserting layouts

There are many layouts in **Single-Frame** category to choose from. They all have the same basic structure; a visible frame containing placeholders and invisible frames that are ready to receive your text(s) and picture(s) and other content, and the number and character of the placeholders within the frames.

In the **Multi-Frame** category, the frames and placeholders are accompanied by lines to create designs that can be used as modern diagrams. These Prezi diagrams may not look exactly the same as traditional diagrams, but if you take a closer look, we are pretty sure you will agree that they are cool and very useful.

Whether you want to insert and use a layout from **Single-Frame** or **Multi-Frame** category, the process is the same.

Getting ready

Now, perform the following steps:

1. Open your prezi.
2. Zoom in on the section of the canvas into which you want to insert content.

How to do it...

1. Click on the **Insert** menu.
2. Choose **Layouts**.
3. This opens the **Layouts** window on the right side of your screen.
4. Click on **Single-Frame** or **Multi-Frame**.
5. Decide which layout to use, and drag it onto the canvas.

As shown in the following screenshot, we inserted three layouts from **Multi-Frame** category to our canvas:

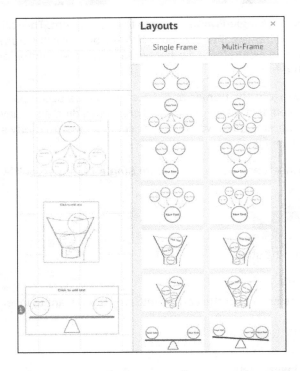

In the preceding screenshot, we selected and dragged three layouts from Multi-Frame category onto the canvas. The collection in Multi-Frame category offers a multitude of diagrams that are useful for a wide variety of illustrations.

> Layouts are actually just frames with content. When inserted in the canvas, these frames are added to the path lane at the end of the path. Edit the order of the path lane if necessary.

There's more...

Why are we so excited? Because Prezi and diagrams are the perfect couple! The reason is that with Prezi you can begin by showing your audience a complete diagram. Then you follow up by zooming in on an interesting detail as you explain this detail. Finally, you can move around in your diagram if you need to cover many details of importance.

If you don't find a diagram that fits your needs exactly, you can easily customize the diagrams because they are created with basic graphic elements and tools such as frames, text elements, lines, and arrows.

Customizing layouts

All layouts are created by combining a variety of frames, text elements, arrows, and lines. This makes the Prezi diagrams very easy to customize.

Want to add or delete a text element? Easy! Need to make a time line longer? Thinking of adding another circle frame to a diagram? You can! Just by re-arranging items on the canvas and adding or removing frames, lines, and arrows, you can adjust any diagram to fit your needs exactly.

Now take a look at the following screenshot, where the layout of **Multi-Frame** category is shown in original version and after editing:

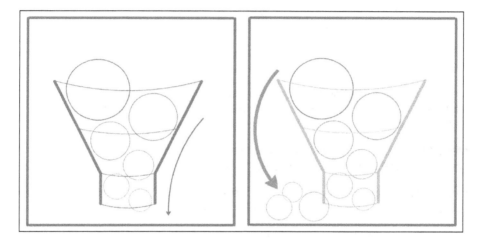

To make this layout fit our needs exactly, we added frames by copying, deleted the blue arrow, added a red arrow, and changed the color of the lines that create the container from blue to green.

When you add elements to a diagram, we highly recommend that you use duplicating (*Ctrl + D*) or copy and paste (*Ctrl + C* and *Ctrl + V*) when adding (more of) the existing elements. This is by far the easiest way to get the sizes and design right when adding elements to a Prezi diagram.

Inserting tables and graphs created in Word and Excel

If you ever need a table for your prezi, you can begin creating tables by inserting, editing, and combining a number of Prezi lines. And if you need to import numbers and data from your spreadsheet program to show them on an elegant graph or in a diagram more sophisticated than Prezi's multi-frame layouts, fire up your engine and get some of those arrows, lines, and texts going.

However, this sounds time-consuming, doesn't it? Well, that's because it is!

You can create tables or graphs in Prezi from scratch, but if your material is complicated or extensive, you will be better off using a program that is designated for that specific material or task and then importing the result into Prezi.

Using MS Word or another word processor allows handling text and tables in many great ways. Why not benefit from that?

Programs such as MS Excel and other spreadsheet programs are specifically designed to handle data and numbers, which is why they do it very well, including converting data and numbers into graphs and elaborate diagrams. Why not use it?

Fortunately, it is not complicated to import material from such programs because they allow you to save files in the PDF format. This is very helpful because PDFs work well in Prezi.

PDFs have a very high resolution, which means that they look great on the Prezi canvas, whether you are zooming out to an overview or in to a detail in your table or graph.

This makes it easy for you to combine the best of two worlds; Prezi for presenting, and Microsoft Office products for creating your material.

Sounds good? Let's get started!

Inserting tables created in Word

It is possible to create tables in Prezi by combining lines and frames.

However, it could be time-consuming due to the large amount of editing this task entails, in order to make the design look nice and unified. Just imagine all those lines that need to have the exact same length!

On most occasions, we (the authors) create our tables in word processors such as MS Word or Pages. We think you should consider it too; it could be easier, and will probably look a lot better on your canvas.

Getting ready

Now, perform the following steps:

1. Open a document in your word processor and create a table.
2. Save the document as a PDF.
3. Open your prezi.
4. Zoom in on the section of the canvas into which you want to insert the table.

How to do it...

1. Click on the **Insert** menu.
2. Choose **From File (PDF, video)...**.
3. Locate the PDF in your filesystem.
4. Select the PDF file and click on **Open** or **Insert** (depending on your computer).

As shown in the following screenshot, use the **Insert** menu to insert a PDF file onto the Prezi canvas:

You cannot edit a PDF in Prezi. If you need to make changes to your table, you must go back to the word processor, make the changes needed, and then save the document as a new PDF.

Inserting graphs or diagrams created in Excel

We love the diagrams that Prezi offers in the **Multi-Frame** category. However, inserting large amounts of data into them will of course be time-consuming. So if you already have your material organized in a spreadsheet program such as Excel, we suggest that you use this program to create your graphs and diagrams.

Most modern spreadsheet programs handle large amounts of data easily, and offer a huge variety of designs and looks for your data.

All you have to do is save your material as a PDF and then insert it in the Prezi canvas.

Getting ready

Now, perform the following steps:

1. Open an Excel file and create a table or graph.
2. Select your table or graph.
3. Save the file as a PDF.
4. Open your prezi.
5. Zoom in on the section of the canvas into which you want to insert the data.

How to do it...

1. Click on the **Insert** menu.
2. Choose **From File (PDF, video)...**.
3. Locate the PDF in your filesystem.
4. Select the PDF file and click on **Open** or **Insert** (depending on your computer).

As shown in the following screenshot, use the **Insert** menu to insert a PDF file onto the Prezi canvas:

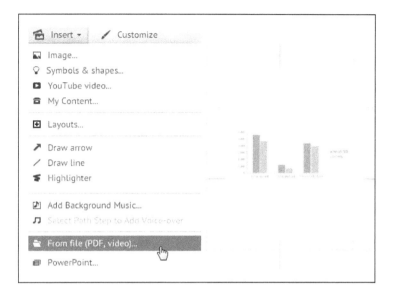

10
Media Files in Prezi

In this chapter, we will cover the following recipes:

- ▶ Audio in Prezi
- ▶ Adding audio to one or more steps
- ▶ Adding background music
- ▶ Audio file types in Prezi
- ▶ Video in Prezi
- ▶ Video file types in Prezi
- ▶ Tips for recording audio
- ▶ A prezi video

Introduction

Media (audio and video) is an important part of many presentations.

Prezi offers the option of inserting audio files into a prezi. In Prezi, we can insert two kinds of audio content: recorded music and voice-over (speaking).

Music can be used as background music that will play through an entire prezi. Voice-over can be added to steps of your prezi. Both of these options are useful when your prezi is not presented by a presenter but is standalone. Situations that call for this would be, for example, embedding the prezi on a website, or running it at a kiosk at a trade fair.

In today's world of visual communication, videos are an integral part of many presentations, and fortunately, Prezi handles video very well.

Prezi offers two different options for inserting videos. We will teach you both, and tell you when to use which.

This chapter will be a fun chapter to read because media can enhance your presentations in great ways and is so easy to add to your prezi. Just by adding media and a dash of inspiration, you will have come a long way towards a professional-looking prezi that supports your message perfectly. (Psst! You don't know a thing about creating media files? Don't worry! Go to the end of this chapter for information about recording.)

> The very special thing about adding audio to a prezi is that if you know how to use audio, you can make your prezi work (almost) like a video with a regular play button. Sounds cool, right?

Audio in Prezi

There are several ways of benefiting from inserting audio files into your prezi.

Adding a recorded interview to one of the steps in your path is a great way to integrate input from people other than the presenter. This will add a "live feel" and variety to your presentation, which will capture your audience's attention.

Background music added to a presentation can be used to set the tone for a prezi.

Adding voice-over to your prezi's steps is a great option for when you cannot present it yourself, for instance, when you place it on a website or send it to someone as an attachment.

These are just a few examples of how you can easily enhance your prezi using audio files. Using different ways of communicating with your audience creates variety in your presentation. Audio is great for audience. While prezis are highly graphical, some concepts do require more explanation than just a picture and a few written words. To explain more without making your design too heavy, you can add audio and video files.

There's more...

To read more about easy ways to create media files, look for our best tips in the *Tips for recording audio* section.

Adding audio to one or more steps

Adding audio to one or more steps in your prezi is easy.

The main use of this feature is to add speech (voice-over) to your prezi. You can add speech to one step, many steps, or all steps.

Creating the voice-over files is not complicated either. Basically, all you need is a cell phone or another simple recording device. Obviously, if you have the option of choosing a more sophisticated recording device, you will get a better quality sound. Some companies even choose to pay for professional speech and recording for important presentations.

But if you need to create something fast or on the fly, it is great to know that you can do it with something as simple as a Smartphone.

Audio files cannot be inserted into a prezi directly from the Smartphone. If you've used a phone to create your audio files, you'll need to send them to a filesystem that is accessible from your computer. This is easily done by e-mailing the audio file to yourself and saving it in your filesystem.

Now, let's get that audio file into the prezi!

Getting ready

1. Open your prezi.
2. Ensure that all frames you want to add audio files to have been added as steps to the path lane (if they are, they will be visible in the path lane).

How to do it...

In the path lane, click on the step you want to add an audio file to. Now that the correct step is selected, proceed using either of these two methods:

1. Open the **Insert** menu.
2. Choose **Add Voice-over to Path Step # X** (number of the selected step).
3. Your filesystem opens up. Locate the audio file.
4. Select **Open** to insert the file.

The alternative method is as follows:

1. Right-click on the thumbnail of the selected step.
2. Choose **Add Voice-over to Path Step**.
3. Your filesystem opens up. Locate the audio file.
4. Select **Open** to insert the file.

Now all you have to do is wait while the audio file loads. Click on the name of the audio file you inserted. This opens a small audio toolbar. You can use this bar to play the audio file or to delete it.

Take a look at the following screenshot, where we show you how to add a voice-over to a selected step using the **Insert** menu, or by right-clicking on the step thumb nail:

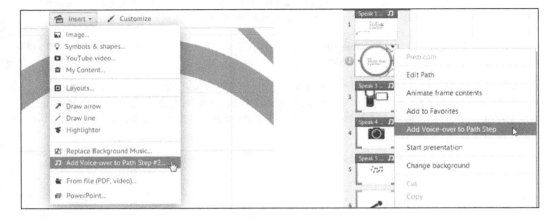

The audio toolbar

When an audio file is added to a step, a black audio file toolbar is added to the step's thumbnail in the path lane. This toolbar makes it easy to see that audio has been added to that step.

Take a look at the following screenshot, where the black audio toolbar shows the name of the audio file that plays on each individual step:

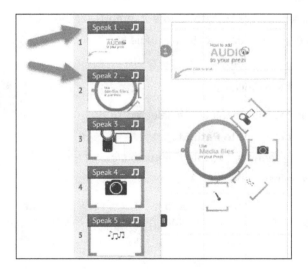

First and foremost, the bar shows the title of the audio file so that you can easily know whether you have picked the right file.

The audio toolbar has other features that make it useful in a number of ways by providing access to information and functions that help you work with the audio file.

How to do it...

1. Hovering over the audio toolbar activates its yellow information tag. This tag provides information about the name, file type, and length of the audio file for the specific step.

2. Clicking on the bar gives you access to functions that allow you to play or delete the audio file. Click on **Done** when finished, as shown in the following screenshot:

 Name your audio files in a way that makes them easily recognizable. You will help yourself a lot by combining keyword names that describe content with the number of the step the file is intended for.

How it works...

Presenting with a prezi that contains audio on one or many steps is not technically different from any other presentations. Just remember that your computer needs some medium of output (speakers) for the sound, and ensure that the volume is not muted (check this before your presentation begins).

When you switch to the **Present** mode, advance through your prezi step by step, by clicking on the forward arrow on your screen or keyboard. As soon as you reach a step that includes an audio file, the audio file will begin playing. Because an audio file works as an integral part of the step, there is no extra clicking involved to play it.

There's more...

Adding an audio file to a step affects the control of that step's duration. A step with no audio file in it will be shown until the presenter clicks on the forward arrow, whereas a step with an audio file in it will be shown through the entire length or duration of the audio file. Consequently, an audio file of 8 seconds will cause a step to be shown for 8 seconds, and an audio file of 30 seconds will cause that step to be shown for 30 seconds.

Some of your steps may contain animations. If a step has only one animation, this animation will appear, the audio file will play until its end, and the prezi will move forward.

But what happens to a step that contains multiple animations? Prezi handles this beautifully, by dividing the available time (the length of the audio file) equally among the animations for that step.

Some people record silence for 2, 4, or 6 seconds (or more) and use that as the sound file for one or more steps. This way of controlling the time spent on a step is helpful if you want to create a video effect in your prezi.

Adding background music

Background music for your prezi presentation can add a very professional touch to it.

Think of music as something you can use actively, to set the right tone for your prezi's message. You can even think of it as a means to priming your viewers' minds so that they will better understand your message.

It is possible to have videos and voice-overs in a prezi even when you are using background music for it. The potential conflicts of sounds are handled like this by Prezi:

- **Video**: The background music stops playing as long as the video is active. When video is over or paused, the background music resumes.

- **Voice-over**: The background music continues to play at a lowered volume for the duration of the voice-over. After the voice-over, the background music's volume is readjusted to the level that was set earlier.

Getting ready

1. Open your prezi.
2. Ensure that your audio's file type is on the list for usable formats (refer to the list in the *Audio file types in Prezi* recipe or to Prezi's website).

How to do it...

1. Click on **Insert**.
2. Choose **Add Background Music**.
3. Navigate to the file of your choice and click on **Open**.
4. Wait while the file loads.
5. When the upload completes, you will see the filename of the background music in a black background music toolbar at the top of the path lane, as shown in the following screenshot:

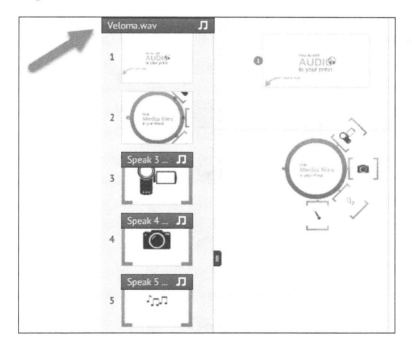

The background music toolbar

When an audio file is inserted into your prezi as background music, a black background music toolbar is automatically added above the path lane.

The background music toolbar shows the title of the audio file that you are currently using for your background music, making it easy to check whether you are using the right file (as shown in the preceding screenshot.)

Finding audio files for your prezi is easy as long as you are prepared to pay for them. There are many sites on the Internet that offer free background music, but many are spams, and even the good ones (http://fma.com/ is a good example) do not allow you to use the free music files for commercial use.

How to do it...

1. Clicking on the bar gives you access to functions that allow you to play or delete the audio file. Click on **Done** when finished.

2. When the mouse pointer is on the bar, it will open a small information tag that shows you the length of the audio file.

There's more...

You can test the background music by clicking on the black banner at the top of the path lane to open the background music toolbar. Click on the play button to listen.

If you want to switch to another audio file for your background music, this is very simple to do. Use the **Replace Background Music** option in the **Insert** menu or right-click on the toolbar.

To delete the background music file, use the trashcan icon in the background music toolbar.

An audio file that is added to a prezi as background music will play until the prezi has fully appeared.

If the prezi lasts longer than the audio file does, the audio file will repeat itself as many times as necessary. Background music automatically fades towards the end of the prezi.

If your prezi includes voice-over (or other audio files) in one or more steps, the background music automatically fades a little whenever you reach a step with voice-over.

 Here is how to create a looping prezi: add a really long piece of background music and choose auto-play when you are in the **Present** mode. Now your prezi will loop as long as the music is playing. Remember the auto-play! A prezi will not loop (replay automatically) just because it contains background music.

Audio file types in Prezi

Prezi works with most common file formats. At the time of writing this book, the file types listed here are compatible with Prezi, but it is always a great idea to check out the Prezi website before spending hours of recording time on a project:

► MP3
► WMA
► AAC
► M4A
► WAV
► MP4
► FLAC
► OGG
► 3GP

 If a file type is causing trouble, try converting it to a WAV file. WAV files always seem to work (Audacity is a good example of a free file converter).

Video in Prezi

Today, the world is full of visual inputs. We see them everywhere, in almost any corner of the world. Using videos in your prezis is great for a variety of reasons, but basically because video is a very strong vehicle for any message.

Imagine your audience watching video footage from an event. Now compare this situation to them watching you talk about that event. It's not hard to tell which of the two will be more engaging, is it?

Think of an interview that would be relevant for your prezi. Again, imagine your audience watching a video of the interview, as opposed to you telling them about it. Again, it's not hard to decide which works better, right?

There are two methods of showing videos in Prezi. The first method includes uploading the video to your prezi; the other method is to access a video that is stored online. We will show you both.

Inserting a video from online storage

YouTube and Vimeo are great places for storing your videos online. The videos are accessible from anywhere, provided you have Internet access, and sharing is easy.

Videos that are stored online in such places can be easily shown in your prezi once you follow this recipe.

Note that the online videos will not be uploaded to your prezi. With this method, Prezi opens a special video player window that you can use to show the chosen video, which has to be stored online first.

To show videos that are stored online (rather than uploaded to the prezi), you are required to be online when presenting.

Getting ready

1. Open your prezi.
2. Open a second tab in your browser. Go to YouTube (or Vimeo). Find the video you want to insert into your prezi.

Videos from YouTube and Vimeo are inserted by navigating to **Insert** | **YouTube video**, as shown in the following screenshot:

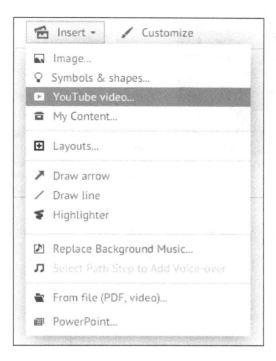

How to do it...

1. In the YouTube or Vimeo tab in you browser window, access the sharing function to copy the video's URL.
2. In your Prezi, open the **Insert** menu.
3. Choose **YouTube** from the menu (this works for Vimeo as well).
4. Paste (_Ctrl_ + _V_) the URL that you copied in the slot provided in the dialogue box.
5. Click on **OK**.

In the following screenshot, we are copying the URL for a YouTube or Vimeo video using the **Share** function for each media respectively:

 For videos stored on Vimeo, you can alternatively download the video file and use the method we will cover now to insert the video.

See also

The second method of inserting videos in Prezi is by uploading a video file into the prezi. This will allow you to present offline with the video. See the next section for this recipe.

Inserting a video from your filesystem

It is not hard to upload video files to your prezi. The great benefit of this method is that it allows you to present and show your videos without being online and without relying on outside servers (such as YouTube's or Vimeo's servers).

For these reasons, we (the authors of this book) prefer to upload our videos into the prezi.

The downside is that if you upload too many video files to a prezi, the prezi may take longer to load before playing, and it tends to react more slowly when presenting. The key is to balance the amount of content so that it matches the prezi's capability to handle it. There are no set numbers for this balance as it will depend on the amount of content in your prezi and the individual sizes of the videos.

Getting ready

1. Open your prezi.

How to do it...

1. Click on **Insert**.
2. Choose **From File (PDF, video) ....**.
3. Select a video. Then click on **Open**.
4. Give the prezi some time to load.

Take a look at the following screenshot:

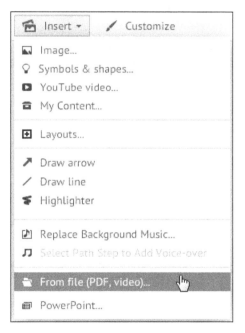

There's more...

If the video file is a step on the path, the video will play automatically when you reach that step in **Present** mode.

If the video file is placed in a frame and this frame is added to the path, the video will not play automatically. To start a video in a frame, you can either add the video to the path as the step after the frame it is in, or manually click on the video's play button to start the video.

If your prezi also has background music, the two soundtracks (background music and video file) will be playing simultaneously.

If your video file type is not in the following list of compatible file types, you can use a video file converter. Prezi recommends `zamzar.com`, and also recommends converting incompatible file types to FLV files.

Video file types in Prezi

By allowing us to use a wide variety of video file formats, Prezi has made it easy for us to use video as an integrated part of any prezi.

The following is the list of all the video formats that will work:

- ▶ FLV
- ▶ F4V
- ▶ MP4
- ▶ MOV
- ▶ MPG
- ▶ M4V
- ▶ WMV
- ▶ MPEG
- ▶ 3GP

The maximum size of a video that you can upload to Prezi is 50 megabytes. Be aware that you may have to edit some videos so that they fit this maximum size.

If the video you want to show in your prezi is stored online (YouTube or maybe a remote server), the size of the video file does not matter. However, we recommend uploading videos to your prezi. This way, you won't have to depend on external servers.

Many great programs for the creation and editing of videos are available for free online.

Creating videos tends to be quite time consuming. Our best tip to help you save some time is to plan ahead. Yep! Sounds a lot more boring than being creative, but it will save you the time taken by retakes and editing.

Plan your content, write a script, and then go!

Tips for recording audio

Most computers, iPhones, Smartphones, and other devices have functions that make it easy to use these devices as recorders or dictaphones. As with anything else, using professional gear creates a higher-quality result. What is right for you depends on the purpose of your prezi. If you aim to be very impressive, your audio quality needs to be top notch. If you are aiming for a somewhat more creative or relaxed style, the relatively unpolished output you get from a less sophisticated recording device may be your best choice.

Recording devices

An audio file created using a Smartphone can be easily mailed to your e-mail account. From there, you can save it in the filesystem on your computer or elsewhere. Save it at a location from where you can access it when you need to insert it into your prezi.

Microphones

If you are using your computer to record, using a microphone with a cord (headset or button microphone) will improve the sound quality. For those looking for top-notch sound quality, we recommend using a USB condenser microphone or visiting a recording studio.

Recording tips

To record a voice-over, experiment with the distance between your mouth and the microphone.

Generally, the sound quality improves when the microphone is closer to the sound source, but a distance that is too short records too much breathing and lip sounds, and too much distance will produce reverberations.

A room with hard walls and lots of space distorts the recording. If possible, choose a small room with softer surfaces.

As odd as it sounds, your car or your closet (preferably with lots of clothes in it) are good places to record, because there will be no reverberation.

Prezi's list of preferred free recording software

Operating System	Software
For Mac	Quick Time (built-in) records M4A
	Audacity (free)
	Audio Hijack (free version)
For Windows	Sound recorder (built-in)
	Audacity (free)
For iPhone	Voice memos (built-in)
For Android	Smart voice recorder (free)
	Easy voice recorder (free)
For Windows phone	Audio Recorder (free)

Editing audio

If you need to edit your sound files, there are several free audio editing programs available. Many of these are great products that work well. You can find them by surfing on the Internet.

Many computers come with program packages that include tools for simple audio editing.

Record your presentation the next time you're in front of an audience (or do it at home). Edit the audio file by dividing it into pieces that match the steps in your prezi. Insert the audio file into Prezi and share your prezi as a link or on a webpage. Now anyone can experience your presentation.

Using a script

If possible, plan your voice-over well ahead and develop a script. The secret of creating a good flow in a prezi is to match the pace of the audio with the visual information. Set a pace that allows the viewer to see and absorb all of the information, without allowing so much time that the presentation becomes boring.

A prezi video

If you add an audio file to every step, your prezi will essentially be displayed (or appear to be) as video.

The prezi shown in the following screenshot has an audio file on each step. Whenever this happens, a play button is added in the prezi's lower-left corner.

This prezi can be played by the viewer in two different ways:

- By clicking on the play button to the left of the black bar under the prezi.
- The usual way—by clicking on the forward arrow at the viewer's desired pace.

All you have to do is to add audio files to every step on your path, and the play button emerges automatically.

There's more...

Consider adding an arrow to your prezi's opening screen to attract your viewers' attention to the fact that this prezi can be played just by clicking on the play button.

If they don't realize this, they can watch your prezi just by clicking on the play button. It's no big deal! Your prezi will work fine simply by the viewer pressing the forward arrow as usual.

 If your prezi has voice-over in all steps but one, it will still have the play button and can be played as a video. Any stop with no audio will be shown for 4 seconds. If you need the time spent on a stop to be longer or shorter, create a silent audio file of the desired length.

11
Templates, Colors, and Fonts

In this chapter, we will cover the following recipes:

- ▶ Choosing the right template
- ▶ Applying a template
- ▶ Customizing the background
- ▶ Applying a theme
- ▶ Customizing templates, colors, and fonts with Theme Wizard
- ▶ Saving your own theme

Introduction

In this chapter, you will learn how to choose, use, and edit Prezi templates.

A template is basically a collection of decorations and settings for your new prezi. These settings define the appearance of frames, and many of them come with beautiful graphics. The template also sets the color of the text elements and controls the fonts in your new prezi.

Templates include various frames, graphics for decoration, and a background color. Using a template makes it easy to create prezis that reflect current trends in color and style. A template works well as the starting point or the foundation of a new prezi.

Templates vary in style as well as in number and organization of frames for your content. In many templates, the graphics and frames are organized so as to help you create a specific type of presentation such as illustrating a conflict, describing a process, illustrating a sequence in time, and other classic themes.

Templates can be used as they are, and they can also be customized easily. Some Prezi users prefer applying the blank template but look at Prezi's templates for inspiration for the design and flow for their prezi.

All prezis are based on templates. Once a prezi has been created, you cannot replace its template.

 Remember that using a Prezi template involves risking that someone in your audience may have used the very same template themselves. This will inevitably make your presentation slightly less impressive. For very important professional presentations, consider creating or shopping for a unique professional design.

When you choose a template or create your own design for a prezi, keep in mind that working with beautiful graphics and interesting fonts might be more fun, but structuring your content correctly is just as important as the look of the presentation. A good structure or flow of your content helps your audience follow your thoughts and understand your message, so be diligent when structuring your content.

See also

To read about the fundamental principles for structuring content, refer *Appendix A, Design* and *Appendix B, Transitions*.

Choosing the right template

Prezi's professional designers often add new templates to the collection. Make sure you check the complete collection every now and then so that you don't miss out on some great new stuff.

The number of templates available varies slightly as some templates are sent to retirement and new ones are added, but there is always a lot to choose from. At present (March 2015), Prezi offers an impressive 90 different templates.

Several factors are important when you choose a template or create a design. Before just falling for some cool design or graphic element (or elements), you need to think about your presentation. Invest a little time in finding the right template.

The graphic style you choose must be a good match for the content as well as the audience. Considering the style of the presenter is a good idea as well. Check out some examples given here for all three aspects:

  ▶ Audience (These could be bankers, investors, creative designers, or students)
  ▶ Content (This could be conflict, romance, timeline, or company strategy)

▶ Presenter's style (This could be funny and free-wheeling, or shy, strictly informative, or anything in between.)

It does not matter how great your prezi is if it is not targeted correctly at your audience. Because the various templates offer different structures, choosing and applying a template that matches your content can be a shortcut to structuring your content right.

In the following image, there are a few screenshots of some examples of Prezi templates that target specific presentation types. Choose a template that is right for your content:

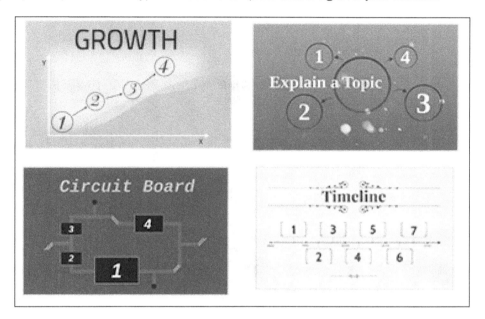

Applying a template

A template defines how everything looks in a particular prezi. You might even say that a template is basically a collection of settings for a file or, in this case, your prezi. All prezis are based on a template. Once a prezi has been created, you cannot apply another template to it.

Every time we create a new prezi, the first thing we need to do is to choose a template. Follow along to see how.

How to do it...

1. Open a new prezi.
2. Click on **Latest** or **More** (bubble **1**) to view the latest or all templates respectively.
3. Notice that every template has a name (bubble **2**).

4. If you want, you can use the search box (bubble **3**) to locate a template by its name. If you don't want to go by names, scroll down to view the collection.

5. Click on **Use template** to apply your chosen template (bubble **4**).

6. Click on **Start blank prezi** to build a prezi from scratch (bubble **5**).

After locating the template that fits your needs, apply for your new template by clicking on **Use template** in the lower-right corner of the following dialog box:

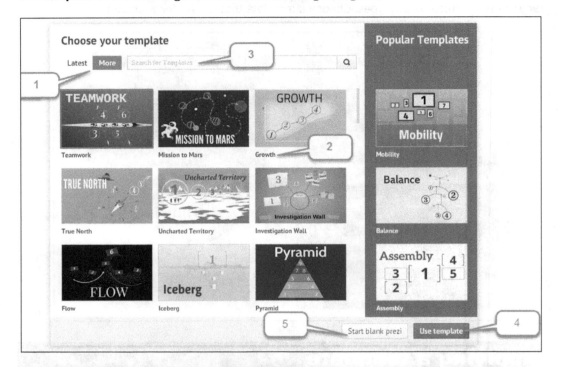

Customizing the background

It is easy to customize the appearance of your prezi. There are many changes we can make to do this. All of these changes will be done in the **Customize** panel. To open this, open the **Customize** menu above the canvas. Some of the tasks we can perform here include changing the background image or applying a theme to our prezi.

In this section, we will look at the relationship among the various visual materials in our prezi. We will then show you how to delete and insert a background image. The panel used to change the background opens to the right of the canvas.

The following screenshot shows you where we go to customize background images (**Change background**) and change theme (**Apply theme**):

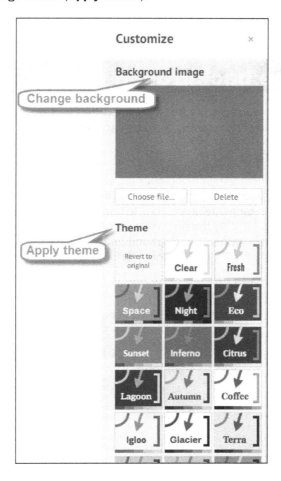

Changing or deleting background color, background image, and graphics

A background image is an image that is integrated with the prezi's background. Items placed on the canvas will float over this background image, creating a 3D effect.

Some of Prezi's templates include not only graphic items on the canvas but also background images. A background image can be inserted, changed, or deleted at any time.

When there is no background image in your prezi, the canvas becomes visible as the background for your prezi.

You can dress up the canvas in any color you like to match your content, style, and taste at any time.

Deleting the background image

Using or deleting a background picture has a big impact on how your prezi looks. Experimenting with deleting and applying pictures can be fun!

Getting ready

To follow along, we recommend opening a new prezi and applying the **Social Network** template. You may use the template search box to find it. Also bear in mind that the collection of templates changes regularly. By the time you read this recipe, you might have to use another template that has a different background image (this can only be checked by applying the template). Take a look at the following screenshot:

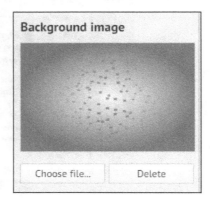

How to do it...

1. Open your prezi.
2. Click on the **Customize** menu to open the **Customize** panel.
3. Click on **Delete** to delete the background image. The canvas is now the background for your prezi's content.

Take a look at the following screenshot, which shows the **Social Network** template before and after deleting the background image:

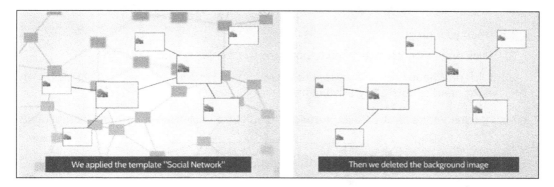

We applied the template "Social Network"   Then we deleted the background image

How it works...

To fully understand what happened in this operation, keep in mind that (potentially) your prezi employs visual material in three different categories:

▶ Background color
▶ Background image
▶ Graphic items on the prezi canvas

In the preceding screenshot, light blue is the background color, the blue business cards form the background image, and the white business cards are graphic items on the canvas. After we have deleted the background image (the blue business cards), only the white business cards (graphic items on the canvas) and the light blue background color are left.

Changing the background image

While the world is full of beautiful images and it is easy to fall in love with something you like, remember that your background image should never take attention away from your content. Fortunately, it is easy to replace one background image with another any time you want to do so.

Remember that you will be zooming into these pictures, often going very close. Obviously, this is going to look better if you are using high resolution images. Images that you want to use for three-dimensional zooming should be large. Interestingly enough, when working with three-dimensional background images, the authors of this book have had the most success using images that exceeded the standard Prezi limit of 2880 x 2880 pixels.

Once you have nice, big images ready, the process is very straightforward. Follow along!

How to do it...

To follow along we recommend opening a new prezi and applying the **Social network** template:

1. Open your prezi.
2. Click on the **Customize** menu to open the **Customize** panel.
3. Click on **Choose file** to access your filesystem and apply one of your image files (you don't need to delete any existing background image).

The background image for the **Social Network** template is shown in the following screenshot:

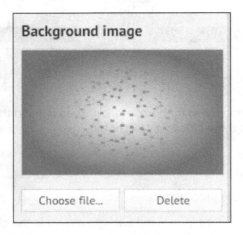

Changing the image file for the background image means changing the graphic item (image of the blue business cards) behind the white business cards. The background image is now a landscape. Behind the landscape, the canvas is still light blue. Changing the background image can make a big difference. Take a look at the following screenshot:

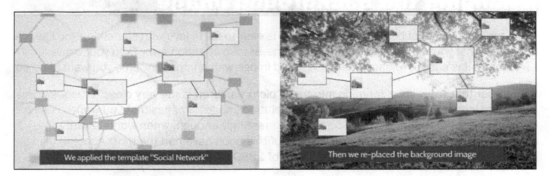

The graphic items on the canvas (the white business cards) and the background (light blue color) are not affected.

Applying a theme

A theme is a set of colors and fonts that you can apply in order to quickly customize your template. Themes are accessed via the **Customize** menu and provide an easy way to customize the look of your Prezi.

It is easy to apply a theme. Once you have opened the **Customize** menu all that you have to do is to click the thumbnail for the theme that you want to apply. Prezi lets you choose from more than 20 different themes. Each theme is stylish and tastefully coordinated by Prezi's professional graphic designers. These are their great choices of readymade or preset looks, which you can apply to any prezi. Themes provide a quick and easy way to customize any template.

Other than being fast, themes provide a means of ensuring that your colors and styles match each other, which helps your prezi look professional. The **Customize** and **Theme** panel opens to the right of the canvas, as shown in the following screenshot:

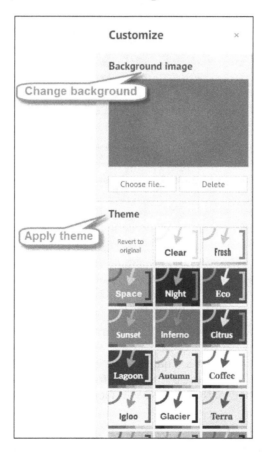

How it works...

Applying a theme impacts your background, frame colors, thickness, and all fonts in your prezi. A theme has no impact on items that are not created in Prezi such as graphic files, videos, and PDF files.

Themes are applied simply by clicking one of the thumbnails in the customization panel. Some themes will impact your template a lot; others won't affect it much (notice that some themes even include characters for writing in Asian languages).

Take a look at the themes shown in the following screenshot that represent a wide variety of styles and looks:

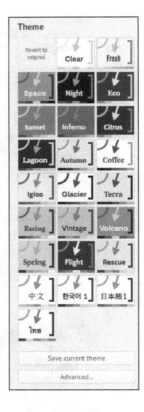

Themes affect only those items that are native to Prezi (in other words, Prezi was used to create them). Native items include the background, frame colors and thickness, all fonts in your prezi, symbols, and shapes. Not all themes affect all the native items that are in a prezi.

 Did you know that you can even create your own themes in Prezi? Read *Saving a customized theme* to learn how to do this.

For this example, we have created a new prezi and chosen a template called **Vital signs**. If you'd like to follow along and try to apply a theme to your own prezi, we recommend that you create a new presentation and apply the **Vital signs** template.

How to do it...

1. Open your prezi.
2. Click on the **Customize** menu to open the **Customize** panel.
3. Click on any of the **Theme** thumbnails.
4. Wait a few minutes while your prezi updates to its new look.

Each theme impacts the look of your prezi in a specific way, as shown in the following screenshot:

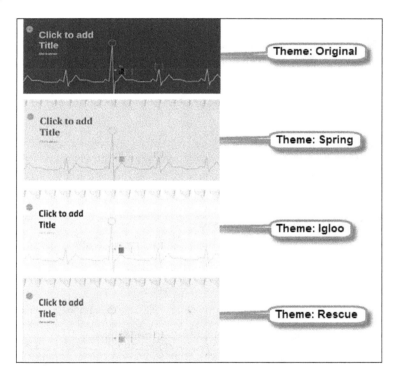

There's more...

Sometimes, you may not like the theme you applied. In that case, just go to the top-left corner of the rows of **Theme** thumbnails in the customization panel. Here, you will find a blank thumbnail with the **Revert to original** text. This is the thumbnail that you'll use if you want to reverse all the changes you made by applying themes. Then you can reapply your template's original look.

Clicking on **Revert to original** only reverts the changes that were applied by the theme. Any other changes you have made to the prezi, such as deleting or inserting graphics, will not be reverted. You can always revert to the original version of your prezi's template.

In the following screenshot you can se the location of *this*:

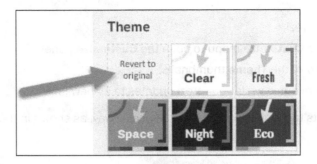

Customizing with Theme Wizard

Theme Wizard is a tool that helps you customize the look of your prezi. It can be used to edit the look of your prezi, whether this has the settings of its template or you have applied a theme.

Theme Wizard makes it easy to apply changes to fonts for your writing styles, colors for your frames, color for the background, arrows, markers, and so on. The changes are easy to make because the wizard organizes all the processes in steps so that you make changes to each item one by one.

Accessing Theme wizard

In this recipe, we will learn how to access the Theme wizard.

Getting ready

1. Click on the **Customize** menu to open the **Customize** panel.
2. Go to the very bottom of the panel, shown in the following screenshot:

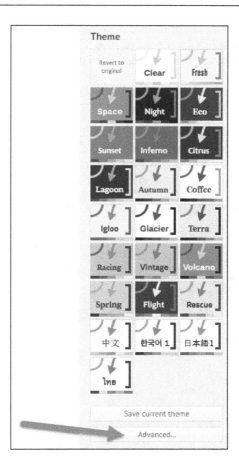

3. Click on the **Advanced** button at the bottom of the **Customize** panel to access the **Theme Wizard**.

The great benefit of the wizard is that you can make behind-the-scene changes with just the click of a button.

Be aware that some of the features that we use in the process of accessing and using the tools to customize the look of our prezi have names that are very similar. The key that we use to open the **Theme Wizard** is called **Advanced**. Once this dialog is open you'll see that it has two keys that you click on to access the editing tools (these keys are marked with red arrows in the following screenshot.) One key is called **Wizard** and the other is called **Advanced**. So the words Advanced and Wizard apply to different features.

For that reason, when we refer to the two keys within the **Theme Wizard** we will use the phrasing Wizard (Wizard dialog key) and Advanced (Wizard dialog key) in order to point out that we are not referring to the dialog box itself, nor to the button in the **Customize** panel. For ease we will shorten (Wizard dialog key) to (Wdk).

We access **Theme Wizards** editing options by clicking on **Wizard** (Wdk) or **Advanced** (Wdk) as shown in the following dialog box:

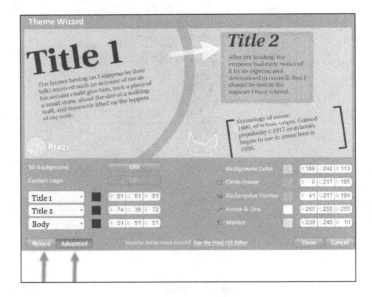

To make it easier to follow the instructions, we will be referring to the **Wizard** key and the **Advanced** key as **Wizard** (editing options) and **Advanced** (editing options).

Every time you make a change, it is reflected in the demo window. The demo window is basically the upper half of the dialog box (our window is green because we applied the Spring theme; your window may show other colors and styles).

Use the demo window to review the changes you made. If you don't like the change you applied, change again or click on **Cancel**. If you like them, click on **Next** to make more changes or **Done** to save and close.

Wizard (Wdk) opens the dialog box for the following edits to be performed:

- Color changes via Prezi's preset color palette
- Creating a three-dimensional background with a single image
- Inserting your own logo (for paid accounts only)

Advanced (Wdk) opens the dialog box for the following edits to be performed:

- Color changes for all Prezi elements via RGB codes
- Creating a three-dimensional background with up to three images
- Inserting your own logo (for paid accounts only)

Some of the options in the two access points (**Wizard** (Wdk) and **Advanced** (Wdk)) are more or less overlapping. As an example, you can establish a three-dimensional background using either **Advanced** (Wdk) options or **Wizard** (Wdk) options. **Advanced** (Wdk) offers the most advanced options.

How it works...

The look of your prezi depends on the template that you chose for your prezi when you created it, as well as on any theme or other changes you may have applied to it. In either case, **Theme Wizard** makes it easy to change colors and fonts so that they match your taste.

We will first explore the options offered via **Wizard** (Wdk). After that, we will explore those offered via **Advanced** (Wdk). There will be a slight overlap, as some of the options are related.

In the prezi, we will be using in this section (refer to following screenshot), we have applied a theme called **Spring**. You may use any template or theme for your prezi if you want to work alongside us for the following sections. Sounds interesting? Well, let's explore the **Theme Wizard** dialog box.

Now, take a look at the following screenshot showing the **Spring** theme:

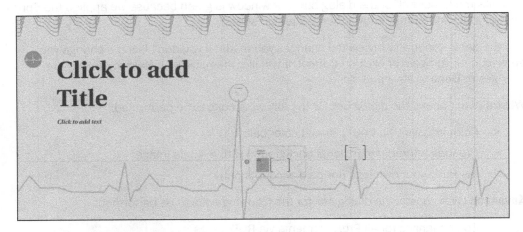

Changing colors with Prezi's default palette

Prezi includes a small palette of colors that you will see often. You'll see it when you change the color for the text elements on the canvas, and in the **Wizard** dialog when working with your background color and many other elements.

Getting ready

1. Open a prezi. It does not matter which template you are using, or whether you have applied a theme.
2. Click on the **Customize** menu to open the **Customize** panel on the right side of the Prezi canvas.
3. Click on the **Advanced** button at the bottom of this panel to open the **Wizard** dialog box.

How to do it...

1. Click on the **Wizard** at the bottom-left corner of the dialog box.
2. You are now on step 1 of the wizard. Here, you can change the background color.
3. Click on any color in the small palette provided. Check the color in the demo window, as shown in the following screenshot:

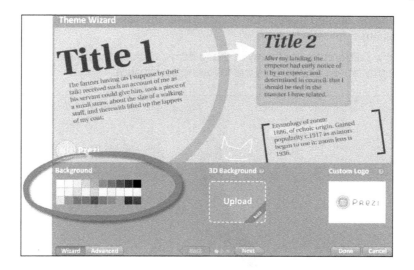

4. If you don't like the color, click on another color in the palette.

5. When you are happy with the color, click on **Next**:

6. You are now on step 2 in the wizard. Here, you can work on the color and fonts for the text.

7. To apply a new color to any of the styles (Title 1, Title 2, or Body); click on the palette next to its label.

8. Check the color in the demo window. Change it again if needed or click on **Next** to proceed to the next step, as shown in the following screenshot:

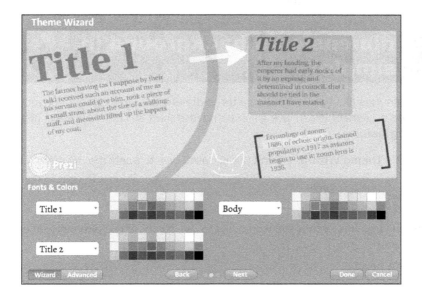

9. You are now on step three in the wizard. Here, you can work on the colors for frames, arrows, lines, and the marker.

10. To apply a different color to any of these items, click on the palette next to their respective labels, as shown in the following screenshot:

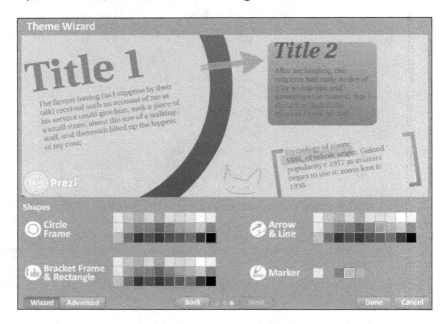

11. Check the color in the demo window. Change it again if needed or click on **Done** to save all your changes and close the dialog.

Three-dimensional background in Prezi (simple)

If you think it sounds like fun working on a three-dimensional background for your prezi, this is easy to do. The makers of Prezi have given us no less than two different ways of working with this interesting feature.

On step 1 in the **Theme Wizard**, we find the simplest way to apply the 3D effect.

Getting ready

1. Find a large image that you would like to use for the three-dimensional effect in your prezi.

2. Open a prezi.

3. Go to the **Theme Wizard** dialog box (navigate to **Custom | Advanced** at bottom of **Customize** panel), which is shown in the following screenshot:

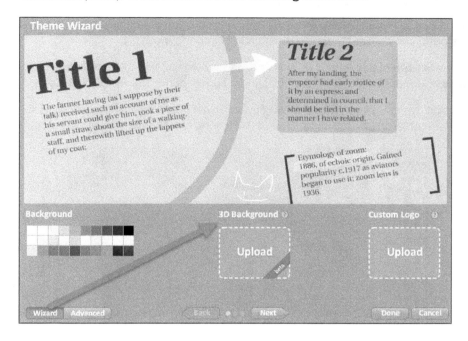

How it works...

The 3D effect is created because the image file (or files) that you upload using the 3D slot becomes an integral part of the background. Afterwards, when you zoom in and out, you will have a feeling that this takes place in a layer above the background, which creates an appealing and lively 3D effect on your canvas.

The image itself does not need to be a special 3D image. The most important feature that it should have is large size because you will be zooming around on it. Interestingly enough, when working with 3D background images, we have had the most success using images that exceeded the standard Prezi limit of 2880 x 2880 pixels.

Also, because the 3D effect is so lively by itself, images that are simple and not too intricate create the best effect.

How to do it...

1. Click on **Upload** below the 3D background label (see the preceding screenshot).

2. Choose a picture in your filesystem and open it.

3. Click on **Done** to finish.

Inserting a custom logo

If you are working professionally with Prezi and have chosen a paid account subscription, you have the option of inserting your own custom logo into the prezi.

The **Theme Wizard** dialog lets us do this in two ways; we can use either **Wizard** (Wdk) or **Advanced** (Wdk) options, both in the bottom-left corner of the **Theme Wizard** dialog.

In this recipe, we are using **Wizard** (Wdk) options. Now take a look at the following screenshot, where we are inserting a logo using **Wizard** (Wdk) in to the **Theme Wizard** dialog box:

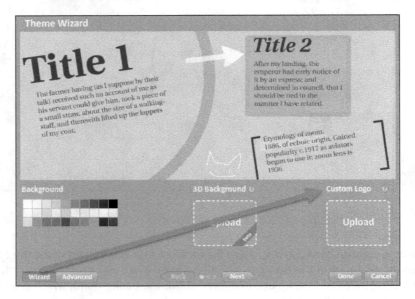

Getting ready

1. Make sure you have a logo available (or some image file that you can use for practice).

2. Open a prezi.

3. Access the **Theme Wizard** dialog (**Custom | Advanced** at bottom of **Customize** panel).

How to do it...

1. Click on **Upload** below the **Custom Logo** background label (see the preceding screenshot).

2. Choose a picture in your filesystem and open it.

3. Click on **Done** to finish.

 Logos that are inserted using one of Prezi's two options are placed in the bottom-left corner of the screen. They will appear on every screen that you will be showing to your audience. To avoid the white square that may appear behind the logo, we recommend that you use a logo that has a transparent background.

Changing colors (advanced options)

Some of the options that you get access to when you click on **Advanced** options and when you click on **Wizard** are overlapping, but the two features do work in their own ways.

When you work with a color in **Advanced** options, you are free to choose whatever color you like, whereas **Wizard** gives you access to a ready-made palette of colors.

How it works...

Advanced option gives you full control of the colors for the text, background, frames, arrow/line, and marker. Changing the colors is easy; just input different values in the slots provided. Click on **Done** when you are satisfied with the colors.

Advanced options hold any color you can dream of; just enter the RGB values that are given in the following screenshot:

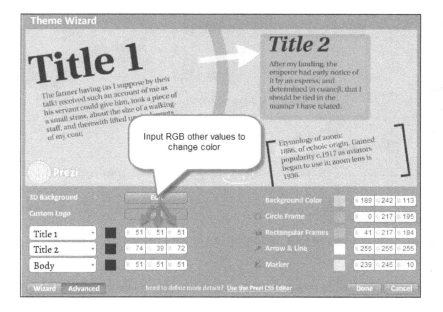

The values you must input are the RGB (Red Green, Blue) color codes. These are codes that define a color by providing information on how much of red, green, and blue needs to be mixed to create a specific color.

This gives you a lot of freedom of color choice because you can input any RGB color code that you like.

RGB color codes are easily found on the Internet. Open any browser and search for "RGB Codes". You will be able to choose from a plenty of overview sheets showing you colors, gradients, and their respective RGB codes.

Items in Prezi tend to be slightly transparent, which causes colors to affect each other when layered. Most of the times, the transparency effect looks pretty cool, but check out the item's overlay-color before you decide the colors for an important presentation.

Three-dimensional background in Prezi – layered (Advanced option)

The more advanced of the two 3D background features offered is what we find in **Theme Wizard** when we use **Advanced** options. This 3D feature allows us to layer our 3D effect:

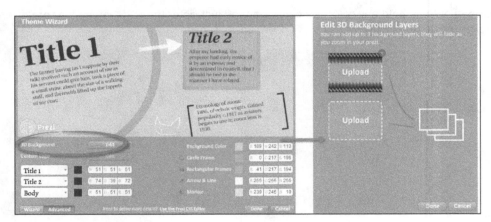

Getting ready

To get started, just click on the **Edit** button circled in the preceding screenshot.

1. Open a prezi.
2. Find the one, two, or three image files that you would like to use for the 3D effect in the prezi.

How it works...

The 3D effect is created because the image file (or files) that you upload using the 3D-slot becomes an integrated part of the background. When you zoom in and out, you will have a feeling that this takes place in a layer above the background, which creates an appealing and lively 3D effect on your canvas.

You can use one, two or three files for the effect. If you use more image files than one, these files will be layered within the Prezi canvas. One image will be visible on top, the second will emerge when you zoom in, and the third will appear on even greater zooms. As always, when you want to zoom close into an image, these image files need to be large files (up to 2880 x 2880 pixels).

 Three-dimensional backgrounds are fun to play with and it cannot be denied that they look cool, but in many cases, the flying feel of a 3D background makes it hard to focus on the content on the canvas, so use them with caution.

How to do it...

1. Click on the **Edit** button next to the **3D Background** label (see the preceding screenshot).
2. Click on **Upload** to upload one or more images.
3. Click on **Done** to finish, as shown in the following screenshot:

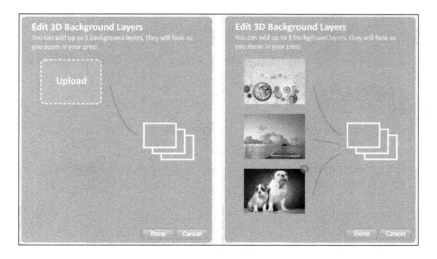

The image uploaded using the top slot will be your top layer. The second image will be in the second layer and it will be visible when you zoom in. The image that you upload via the bottom slot will be in the third layer, emerging only when you zoom in further.

Inserting a custom logo (Advanced option)

If you are working professionally with Prezi and you have a paid account, you have the option of inserting your own custom logo into the prezi.

The **Theme Wizard** dialog lets us do this in two ways; we can use either the **Wizard** (Wdk) or the **Advanced** (Wdk) option, both in the lower-left corner of the **Theme Wizard** dialog.

In this recipe, we are using **Advanced** (Wdk) option. In the following screenshot, we are inserting a custom logo using **Advanced** (Wdk) option in the **Theme Wizard** dialog box:

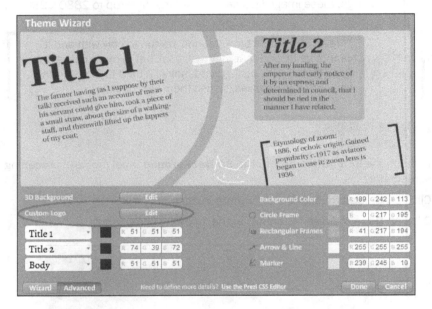

Getting ready

1. Make sure you have a logo available (or some image file that you can use for practice).
2. Open a prezi.
3. Access the **Theme Wizard** dialog (navigate to **Customize | Advanced** button at bottom of **Customize** panel).

How to do it...

1. Click on **Edit** to the right side of the **Custom Logo** label (circled in the preceding screenshot).
2. Choose your logo or another image file in your filesystem and open it.
3. Click on **Done** to finish.

Logos that are inserted using one of Prezi's two options are placed in the bottom-left corner of the screen. Furthermore, the logo appears on every screen that you will be showing your audience. If you want more control over where and when to show your logo, insert it on the canvas as you would do with any other image. Then place and size it according to your liking.

Changing fonts in your prezi

All the templates in Prezi come with three different styles for text. These styles are called Title 1, Title 2, and Body.

A style is a collection of settings for text. Each collection or style is fashioned to match the template of which it is a part. This is why the three styles look different from one template to another.

It is easy to change the font of any of the three styles. Use **Theme Wizard** to access Prezi's beautiful fonts.

 All other changes to styles are applied by opening the text's textbox on the Prezi canvas, where you can make selections such as Bold, Italic, and so on. It is only for changing the font that you need to access the **Wizard** dialog.

In the following screenshot, you can see the selection of fonts that Prezi offers. While the selection is not huge, it is actually a great selection. It offers a variety of styles that will help you choose the right look for a presentation for bankers, your local flower show, or the end-of-the-year office party:

Alegreya
Aleo
Arimo
Arsenal
Cabin
DOMO ZINE OT
From Where You Are
Heuristica
KG Empire of Dirt
KOMIKA TITLE
League Gothic
Liberation Mono Pr
Noto Sans
Playfair Display
Tinos
Titillium

The list of fonts that you just saw shows the complete selection of fonts in Prezi, whether you are looking for a new font for your titles, subtitles, or body text.

Getting ready

1. Open a prezi. It doesn't matter which template you are using or whether you have applied a theme.

2. Click on the **Customize** menu to open the **Customize** panel on the right side of the Prezi canvas.

3. Click on the **Advanced** button at the bottom to open the **Theme Wizard** dialog, as shown in the following screenshot:

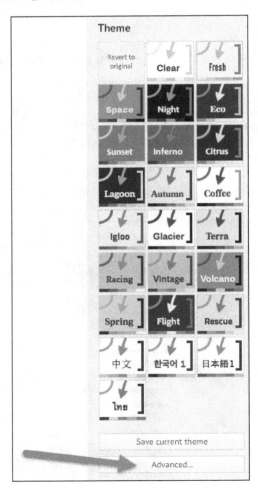

How to do it...

1. Click on the **Wizard** button in the bottom-left corner of the **Theme Wizard** dialog.

2. You are now on step 1 in the **Theme Wizard**. Click on **Next** to proceed to step 2.

3. Click on the white box for **Title 1**, **Title 2**, or **Body** to view the font selection.

4. Click on the font you want to apply. Then check it out in the demo window. If you don't like the font, reopen the font selection and apply another font.

5. When you are happy with the font, click on **Done** to save and close.

Take a look at the following screenshot, where we are using **Theme Wizard** to change the font for the writing styles:

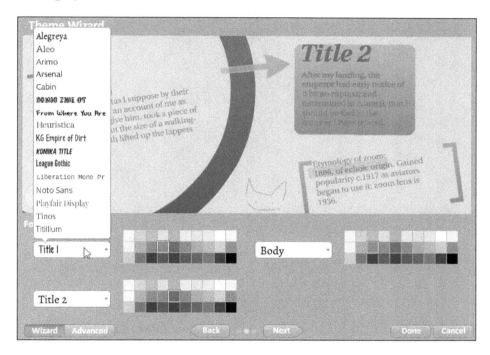

Saving a customized theme

After applying new colors for your frames, choosing other fonts for your styles, and looking up that RGB code for the background, wouldn't it be great if you could save your settings? Well, you can—and very easily too!

Saving a customized theme preserves all the settings that are currently in your prezi. With a customized theme, these settings can be applied to any prezi by a click of a thumbnail. We'll show you how.

How to do it...

1. Apply the changes to your prezi using the **Theme Wizard** dialog.
2. Click on **Save current theme** in the **Customize** panel.
3. Check out the new thumbnail (your new theme) at the bottom of the **Customize** panel.

Take a look at the following screenshot:

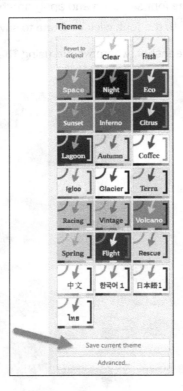

You can save and keep up to five customized themes. If you need to delete a theme to make room for another, just hover over the thumbnail and click on the red circle in the top-right corner, as shown in the following screenshot:

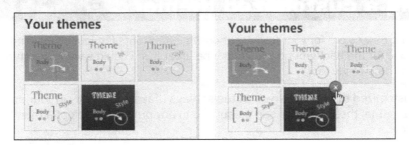

12
Presenting with Prezi

In this chapter, we will cover the following recipe:

▶ Prezi in present mode

Introduction

When you are out there looking at your audience, looking forward to showing your prezi, feeling well prepared (yep! You rehearsed!), and so ready, that's what it's all about—that's when your prezi comes to life.

Prezi's presenting features support all kinds of presenters. Whether you prefer a detailed plan and a strict path for your prezi or you want to use a looser, improvisational style, you will find that Prezi is the tool for you.

Mastering Prezi's presenting features is a must for a successful presentation. Fortunately, these features are easy to learn and understand, making it possible for all presenters to feel at home in these functions.

This chapter covers all the functions in Prezi's present mode.

See also

You can download a portable Prezi—a file type designed just for presenting. If you need to refresh your memory on this topic, please read *Chapter 15, Sharing and Collaborating*.

 Connecting to a projector requires a special cable; be sure to bring it.

Prezi in present mode

To navigate your prezi while presenting, you have several choices. Some prefer to use a mouse, others swear by their remote control, while a few may prefer to use their keyboards (we don't recommend this; it's cumbersome).

Whatever your tool is, you need to know the features of Prezi's present mode, from the simple forward and backward stepping to the functionalities that will allow you to move freely around the canvas while presenting.

So, here's to Prezi in present mode:

Getting ready

1. Open your prezi.
2. Click on **Present** in the top-right corner of the screen.
3. Prezi goes fullscreen showing the message, "Prezi is now full screen".
4. Wait a few seconds and the message disappears.
5. The presenting tools appear on the Prezi screen.

To get an overview of the controls that you will use for presenting, take a look at the following screenshot, where the numbers **1** to **4** show the location of the presenting controls:

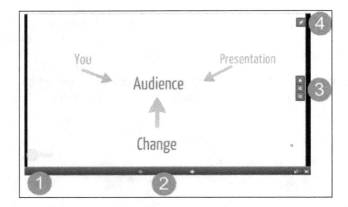

The presenting tools are as follows:

1. Navigate to other slide.
2. Forwards/Backwards.
3. Home / zoom in / zoom out.
4. Back to edit mode.

Knowing the presenting features really well will help you feel at ease while presenting with your prezi, so invest a few minutes in preparing for success.

 If you need your prezi to play automatically, use the autoplay feature in the lower-right corner of the Prezi screen to automatically show your steps for 4, 10, or 20 seconds. Read more about this in the *Prezi in autoplay* section.

How to do it...

Here you will learn how to handle the **Present** mode controls and use the autoplay function of Prezi.

Present mode controls

The present mode controls are visible when you switch to present mode.

These controls fade out after a few seconds but will reappear when you move your mouse to the bottom or right side of the canvas in present mode.

1. **Move to any path stop**: When you hover your mouse over the lower part of the screen, a blue bar with a blue ball will appear. Drag the ball to the right (forward) or left (backwards) to view thumbnails of the stops on your path (shown in the preceding figure). Release the ball when on the stop you want, and Prezi moves to this specific stop. The following screenshot shoes the blue bar that is seen when you hover your mouse. Drag the blue ball to move fast between thumbnails of stops.

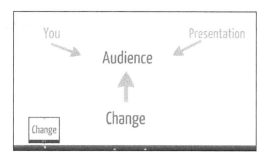

2. **Move forward or backward on the path**: Click the arrows at the bottom of the present screen by using your mouse or a remote control. You may also use the right/left arrows on your keyboard, or the spacebar (forward move only).

3. **Move to overview of complete prezi**: Hovering your mouse on the right side of the screen produces the **Home** button (house icon). Click on it to zoom the presentation out to an overview of all content on the presentation canvas. Here, you will also find the magnifying glasses that you may use to zoom in or out.

4. **Exit the presentation**: Clicking on the pencil icon in the top-right corner takes you back to **Edit** mode. Alternatively, you may hit the *Esc* key. This too takes you to **Edit** mode.

> Using your keyboard or a remote clicker makes the black navigation bar at the bottom of the screen disappear for a better view of your beautifully designed prezi.

Prezi in autoplay

Prezi has an autoplay function that is very handy if, for example, you want your prezi to run continuously at a stand at a trade fair. A presentation set to autoplay will run continuously, by restarting from stop 1 after having shown all the other stops. It will run until you stop it. Click the autoplay icon to have your prezi play and loop automatically, as shown in the following screenshot:

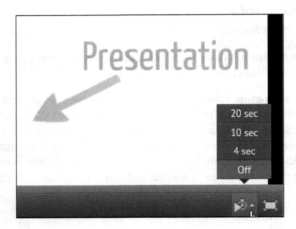

The autoplay icon is the stop watch at the bottom of the present mode screen. Click on this icon to reveal a list of possible time settings, and click to choose if every stop should be shown for 4, 10, or 20 seconds.

There's more...

Elements on the canvas can be accessed quite easily, if you need to zoom in on a detail. The following table shows you how. Understanding how easy it is to deviate as well as returning back to your path when presenting, gives you a lot of freedom as a presenter.

The last row in the table shows you how to return to your last path stop where you left off to zoom in your series of steps (the path).

In present mode, if you:	Prezi will:
Click on an element (text, image, video)	Zoom to that specific element
Click on a group	Zoom to the group
Click on a frame	Zoom to show that specific frame
Click outside a frame	Zoom to the nearest surrounding frame
Click on a forward arrow	Take you back to the last path stop you visited

Knowing these action/re-action schemes well allows you to move more freely in your prezi when you are presenting. It also looks cool and professional, so give it a few minutes of your time.

 If you ever get lost on your canvas, remember that the **Home** icon to the right side of the screen zooms out to an overview of everything on your canvas.

See also

To learn the principles for a good path for your prezi, please read *Appendix B, Transitions*.

13
Prezi on Other Devices

In this chapter, we will cover the following recipes:

- ► Using Prezi offline—Prezi for Windows/Mac
- ► Working in Prezi for Windows/Mac
- ► Synchronizing your prezis
- ► Re-synchronizing your prezis
- ► Detaching a prezi from your online Prezi account
- ► Working online or offline in Prezi—the differences
- ► Prezi on iPad and iPhone
- ► Downloading a prezi to your device
- ► Editing and closing a downloaded prezi
- ► Presenting with Prezi on an iPad

Introduction

Prezi is a tool that is available online. Typically, we access Prezi using our favorite browser. Using this browser, we create and edit our prezis. We store them in our Prezi account where they are available for as long as we need. When we need to present our prezi, we do it while we are online or use the portable prezi that we created. Easy!

But did you know that Prezi also comes with a program that can be downloaded to your computer? This program is called **Prezi for Windows** and **Prezi for Mac**. This program is the same tool that we can access in the online version, and it comes in very handy if you need to work on your prezis without being online (such as in trains, planes, and so on).

Prezi for Windows/Mac is part of the Pro account, which means that it is a feature for which you will have to pay extra. But since any Prezi account comes with a 30-day free trial of Prezi for Windows/Mac, it is easy to test before you buy.

If you are the owner of a Smartphone or an iPad or iPad, you have a third option for creating, editing, and showing your prezis. This option is the Prezi app that you can download into your Smartphone or iPad. This app is free.

In this chapter, we will work with Prezi for Windows/Mac and Prezi for Smartphone/iPad.

See also

Not sure which account to choose? Read more about the various accounts in *Chapter 1, Administer Your Account and Your Prezi*.

By downloading your prezi in a format called *Portable Prezi*, you can present offline even if you do not have a Pro account. You can read about portable prezis in *Chapter 15, Sharing and Collaborating*.

Using Prezi for Windows/Mac

Using Prezi for Windows/Mac gives you access to create, edit, and present with Prezi even if you are offline.

The online and the offline versions of Prezi are almost similar, but we will (of course) describe the differences, and we're also going to make it easy for you to understand how to synchronize your prezis between the two versions.

Of course, it all begins with you downloading the program into your computer, so that's where we begin.

Getting ready

Log in to your Prezi account online.

How to do it...

1. Click on the **Download Prezi for Windows** link below the list of folders.
2. Follow the instructions for your operating system.

   Prezi for Windows/Mac is now installed on your computer.

3. Open and use Prezi on your computer.

We can install Prezi on your computer by the click of a button, as shown in the following screenshot:

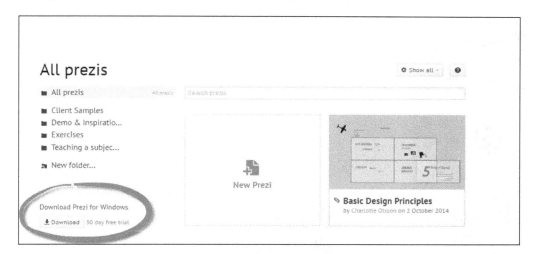

 All Prezi accounts offer the option of trying Prezi for Windows/Mac for a 30-day period at no cost. Try it out! It's a great program.

Working in Prezi for Windows/Mac

Working in Prezi for Windows/Mac is largely the same as working in Prezi online. Only a few things are different. (We'll tell you about those in the *Working online or offline in Prezi – the differences* section.) Here, we'll take a look at how to get started working with Prezi offline.

How to do it...

1. Install Prezi for Windows/Mac as described earlier.
2. Locate and click on the Prezi icon in your programs folder or in your taskbar.

The following is a screenshot of what you see when you open Prezi for Windows/Mac:

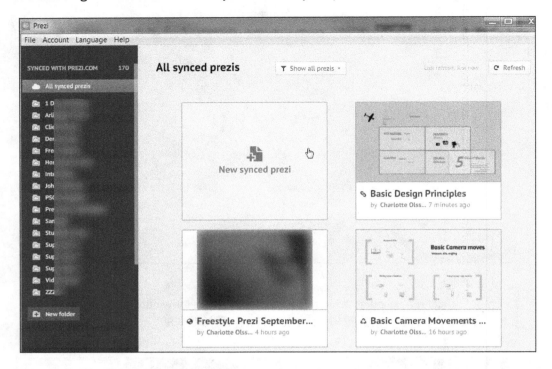

When you open Prezi for Windows/Mac, an overview window shows all your prezis.

Prezi for Windows/Mac opens, showing an overview of all the prezis you have on your computer and in your online account.

To the left, you'll find the folders that you created online for your prezis. The folders work exactly as they do online, and you can create new folders the same way as you do online (by clicking on the **New folder** button below the list of folders).

Synchronizing your prezis

If you take a closer look at the preceding screenshot, you'll notice that the icon for the red prezi looks blurred. This is Prezi's way of telling the user that this prezi has not been synced to reflect the changes that have been applied to its online version. Fortunately, this is an easy fix.

How to do it...

Synchronizing a prezi is easy.

1. Hover over the blurred prezi's thumbnail.
2. Click on the **Download** button that appears.
3. The blurriness will roll off and now your prezi is synced to match the online version.

 Prezis that are created or edited using Prezi for Windows/Mac will be synchronized with your online Prezi account as soon as your computer connects to the Internet.

Re-synchronizing your prezis

If you have been editing a prezi on `http://prezi.com/` or a new prezi has been shared with you, clicking on **Refresh** synchronizes all your offline prezis with their updated online version (you must be working on a computer connected to the Internet for the refresh to work).

Take a look at the following screenshot:

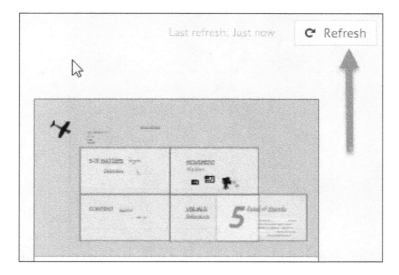

Prezis that are downloaded onto your computer are accessed via the overview window in Prezi for Windows/Mac.

Detaching a prezi from your online Prezi account

All prezis in your main overview window in Prezi for Windows/Mac will be synced as soon as you click on the **Refresh** button.

Sometimes, this is not what you want, maybe because a prezi is your specific version of a more generic presentation. Or there may be an online prezi that you decide to not store online any longer for security reasons.

If you need to store a prezi on your computer only, and it is not to be synced with your online account, we recommend downloading the prezi and saving it as a prezi file. This file format is called `pez`.

How to do it...

Creating a `.pez` file in **Prezi for Windows/Mac** is easy:

1. Hover over the lines icon on the top-right corner of the prezi's thumbnail.
2. Choose **Export to prezi file (.pez)**.
3. Pick a location in your filesystem for the prezi to be stored.

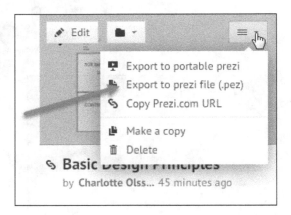

4. Later, when you are working in **Prezi for Windows/Mac** and need to access your `.pez` file, use the **Import a prezi** command that is located just below the list of folders.

5. If the pez file is based on a prezi that was not originally created in your online account, it is now on your computer only as a local prezi (unlike the downloaded prezis that are also online). Local prezis are accessed by clicking on **All local prezis** below the list of folders to the left, as shown in the following screenshot:

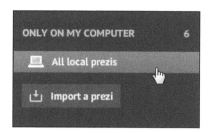

 A local prezi is stored on your computer but not online.

There's more...

The `.pez` format is very useful for several reasons. People save their prezis as `.pez` files to avoid storing sensitive information online, or to be able to send an editable prezi to a colleague who also uses **Prezi for Windows/Mac**. The file format also works great if you want to bring an editable presentation with you on a USB drive.

You can read more about `.pez` files in *Chapter 15, Sharing and Collaborating*.

Working online and offline in Prezi – the differences

As you may already know, working in Prezi online and offline is pretty much the same. There are only three differences:

▶ The user interface in **Prezi for Windows/Mac** is similar to the user interface for Prezi online, except for one thing—the **Exit** (actually it exits and saves) button that is in the top-right corner of the online Prezi window. Here, in **Prezi for Windows/Mac**:

   ❑ Saving is done by clicking on the **Save** icon
   ❑ Exiting is done by clicking the **X** in the top-right corner (Windows) or top-left corner (Mac).

As shown in the following screenshot, click on **Save** to save (1) and click on **X** to exit (2) your prezi in Prezi for Windows:

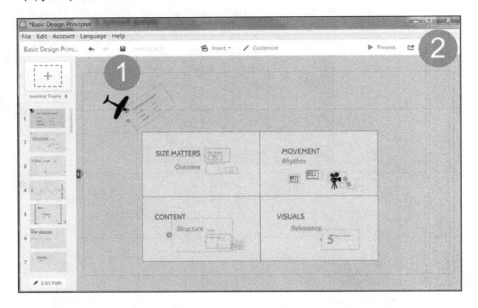

- ▶ When you are working in **Prezi for Windows/Mac** and are inserting a video file or a PDF file into your prezi, the program automatically goes online to Prezi.com to perform a conversion of the video or PDF file to a format that works for **Prezi for Windows/Mac**. You are prompted with a message that asks you to allow this conversion. If you want the video or PDF file in your offline prezi, you need to allow the conversion.

- ▶ Elements that you store in **My content** when you are working offline are not (in fact, never) synced with your online **My content** collection, but are stored only locally (on your computer).

 To store elements from an offline prezi to your online **My content** collection, go online, open the prezi that has the content and store it to your online account's **My content**.

Prezi on iPad and iPhone

If you like using Prezi while you are on the go or if you sometimes need to present without letting your computer use online prezis or Prezi for Windows/Mac, chances are that you will enjoy the Prezi app.

The Prezi App is available for free. The app makes it easy to download your prezis and take them with you to present anywhere, even without a connection to the Internet. As always, when you choose to present offline, remember that links, online videos, and so on will not be accessible.

After downloading your prezis, use the app for presenting and perform basic editing on your prezis. This app is available for both iPads and Smartphones.

How to do it...

1. Locate the "Prezi for iPad / Smartphone (Android or iphone)" app online.
2. Download the app.
3. Click on **Log in** and fill in your Prezi account information.
4. You will now be logged in to your online Prezi account.
5. After logging in, your prezis will be accessible via your device.

When you open Prezi on your device, you will see an overview window that shows all the prezis that you have in your online account, as shown in the following screenshot:

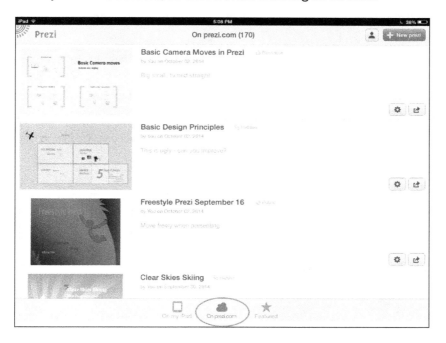

Prezis that are in your online account can be accessed when you are online. If you need to access one or more prezis without being online, you must first download this (or these) to your device.

Downloading a prezi on your device

Sometimes, you might find yourself in a place where your iPad or Smartphone does not have online access. Don't ever let that stop you from showing your beautiful prezis! All you have to do is download the prezis you need when you have online access. Once a prezi has been saved (downloaded) to your specific device, it is available even if you are offline.

How to do it...

It is easy to download a prezi to store it on your iPad or Smartphone:

1. Open the Prezi app.
2. Tap on **On prezi.com** at the top of the overview window to show all your prezis.
3. Scroll down through your prezis to locate what you are looking for.
4. Select your prezi by tapping its thumbnail.
5. The prezi will now start downloading onto your device. This may take a couple of minutes, depending on your Internet connection.
6. Once the prezi has finished loading, it opens in **Present** mode. Tap on the right side of the screen to go ahead with your presentation.

When a prezi has been fully downloaded to your iPad, you can access the presentation under the **On my iPad** tab, as shown in the following screenshot:

Editing and closing a downloaded prezi

Prezi for iPad is not a full-featured Prezi program, and there are a few tasks that you cannot do with it, such as removing a frame from your path without actually deleting the frame, applying themes, using the **Theme Wizard** dialog, and so on. However, it does offer access to the editing features that we use the most, such as adding text, images, and videos, and moving and resizing your content on the canvas. If you need to create a new prezi using your iPad, these features will be available.

How it works...

To access the editing tools, begin by tapping at the top of the **Prezi for iPad** screen. An **Edit** button emerges in the top-right corner. Click on it to begin editing your prezi.

Take a look at the following table showing tasks and actions to be done:

Task	Action
Edit text	Click twice on the text element you want to edit.
Close textbox	Click outside the edited textbox.
Add textbox	Click on **T+** at the right side of the screen.
Select element	Click on the element once.
Resize	Drag the double-headed arrow icon at lower right to resize.
Move	Drag the element to the new position.
Turn	Grab the rotation icon at the bottom-left corner to turn.

Task	Action
Delete	Click on **Delete** in the box above the selected item.
Replace	Click on **Replace** in the box above the selected item.
Save and exit	Click on the **My Prezis** button (top-left corner) to exit the prezi. You will be prompted to accept or decline the changes you made.

 You can create your prezis online or in **Prezi for Windows/Mac** to enjoy all the editing features. Use the editing features in Prezi for iPad if you are on the go and need to modify a presentation.

Now, take a look at the following screenshot:

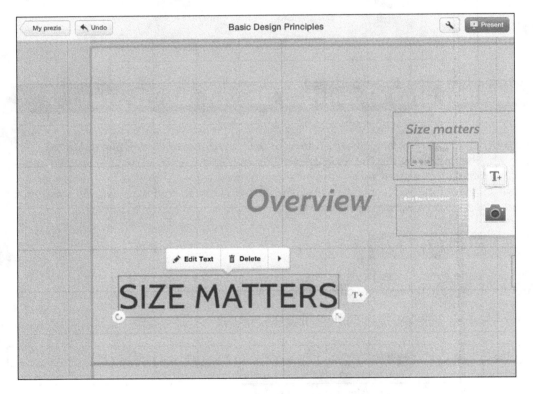

There's more...

Clicking on the camera icon opens the toolbar, as shown in the following screenshot:

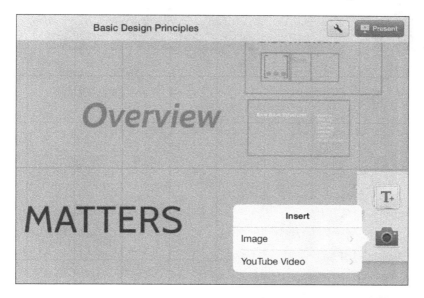

You can use the camera icon to easily insert images and videos from YouTube.

Presenting with Prezi on an iPad

Presenting from an iPad is very convenient because the iPad is so easy to take along with you. While Prezi for iPad is a little limited when it comes to editing, the presenting feature is great and we recommend it warmly.

Presenting on an iPad makes it easy to follow your path, but it is also easy to deviate from the path, because you can swirl and drag the canvas any way you want with your fingertips. Smooth!

How to do it...

1. Click on the **Play** button on the thumbnail of the prezi you need for your presentation.
2. When the prezi has finished loading, it opens in the **Present** mode.
3. Tap on the right or left side of the iPad screen to go forward or backward on the path, respectively.

4. To exit the **Present** mode, click on the upper-right corner of the screen and choose **My Prezis** (to go to the overview of all prezis) or **Edit** to edit a particular prezi. Now, take a look at the following screenshot:

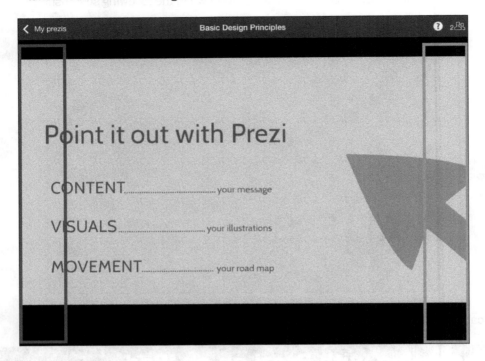

When you are presenting, it is easy to navigate through your presentation. Tap on the area to the left (blue box in the preceding screenshot) to go one step backwards, tap the area to the right (red box in the preceding screenshot) to move one step forward.

There's more...

Further navigation in **Present** mode on the iPad can be done by using the fingertip motions that you may already know:

1. Pinch the canvas in or out to zoom in or out, respectively.
2. Click twice on the item or frame to zoom in.
3. Again, click twice on the item to zoom out.
4. Click twice on the canvas to zoom to the nearest frame.

14

PowerPoint and Prezi

In this chapter, we will cover the following recipes:

- ▶ Reusing PowerPoint material—method 1
- ▶ Reusing PowerPoint material—method 2
- ▶ Reusing PowerPoint material—method 3

Introduction

Even if your older presentations were created in PowerPoint and you are now using Prezi, we bet that some of your presentations include content that you wish you could transfer to Prezi.

And you can! There are three different methods of importing material from a PowerPoint presentation to your Prezi canvas.

Two of these methods are very easy to use. Actually, the third one is easy too, but it entails a certain amount of editing.

Nonetheless, the good news is that it is not a hassle to transfer content from our old friend, PowerPoint, to our new best friend, Prezi. Whether you want to import a single-slide or the complete `.ppt` or `.pptx` presentation, we can help you!

 Did you know that in PowerPoint, you can right-click on almost any item on a single slide and use the menu that opens to save that item as an image? This is very handy, since images are so easily inserted in Prezi.

Reusing PowerPoint material

In the following recipes, we will demonstrate three methods to transfer (copy) material from PowerPoint to your prezi.

Methods 1 and 2 show you how to insert and reuse one or more single slides from a PowerPoint presentation and display them on your Prezi canvas.

Method 3 explains how to use Prezi's import feature for one or all slides from a PowerPoint presentation.

The following screenshot shows our *Supertek Benefits* presentation. This is the PowerPoint presentation that we will be using for this chapter. Because odd things are going to happen to it in the following recipes, we advise you to take a moment to look at it in order to notice the design (the bricks, the red bar, and the white background), position, and appearance of the text elements on the slides (all uppercase headings, red letters, and black letters).

Take a look at the following screenshot showing our PowerPoint file that has a brick background, a red rectangle, and letters in red and black:

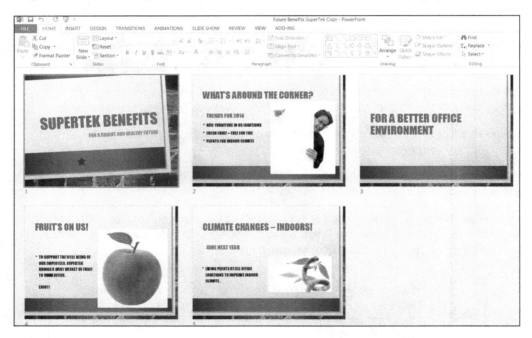

Reusing PowerPoint material – method 1

Most presenters that we've worked with have used PowerPoint prior to becoming Prezi fans. If you have used PowerPoint previously, it is likely that you have a few great PowerPoint presentations that contain slides that you would like to transfer or import to the Prezi canvas, while preserving their appearance.

In this section, we will show you how to perform such an import. We do this by saving our PowerPoint material in PDF format. The PDF document is then easily inserted into the Prezi canvas using the **Insert** menu.

Getting ready

1. Open PowerPoint and then the PowerPoint file that you want in your prezi.
2. In PowerPoint, navigate to **Choose File | Save as**.
3. Choose **PDF** as your file format.
4. Name and save the PDF file.

How to do it...

Now, let's do the transfer to Prezi:

1. In the Prezi, click on **Insert**.
2. Choose **From file (PDF, video)...**, as shown in the following screenshot:

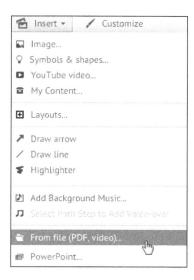

After you've located the PDF document in your filesystem, click on **Open** to insert it. The presentation will now be imported to your canvas. The PDF file will have the same number of pages as the slides in the original PowerPoint file. The PDF file takes a while to load, but it is definitely worth waiting for, since you will have every slide placed on the canvas in front of you in a nice grid that makes it easy to view the imported content.

Take a look at the following screenshot showing our PPT file inserted on the Prezi canvas as PDF pages:

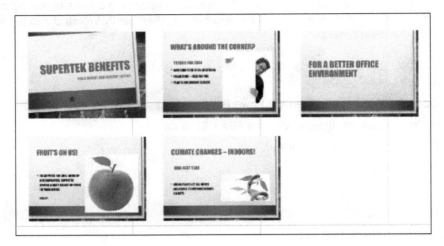

Saving and inserting your PowerPoint as a PDF file preserves the original design and formats from PowerPoint.

How it works...

This method ensures that the design of a slide is kept as it was originally designed in PowerPoint.

At the same time, the downside of using this method (converting to PDF) is that you will not be able to edit any part of the material on the canvas in Prezi. The reason is that PDF files cannot be edited with Prezi.

When a PowerPoint file is saved as a PDF file, each individual slide becomes an individual page. If you don't need all the slides from your original PowerPoint, just delete these PDF pages from the Prezi canvas.

Reusing PowerPoint material – method 2

PDF is a format that works really well in Prezi, but there are many other options. Image formats such as .png and .jpg also look great on the Prezi canvas.

In this section, we will show you how easy it is to save your slides in .jpg or .png format. The images will then be available for your Prezi presentation by navigating to **Insert | Image**.

The main difference between the first method and the second method is that with the first method, you can import only the complete deck of slides from your PowerPoint presentation, whereas in the second method, you have the option of importing individual slides.

Getting ready

1. Open PowerPoint and open the PowerPoint file that you want in your prezi.
2. In PowerPoint, navigate to **Choose File | Save as**.
3. Choose an image file format such as .png or .jpg.
4. Name and save the image file.

You can save all slides or just one, as both options are offered, as shown in the following screenshot:

When you are using this method, you have the option of saving either a selected slide or the complete collection of slides in the presentation.

When you have made your choice to save one slide or all slides and selected a destination, PowerPoint creates a folder that it will name after the PowerPoint presentation. In it, the slides that you chose to save will be available as individual image files. An information dialog box appears, as shown in the following screenshot:

How to do it...

1. Open your prezi.
2. In the prezi, click on **Insert**.
3. To insert slides that are saved as images, choose **Image**, as shown in the following screenshot:

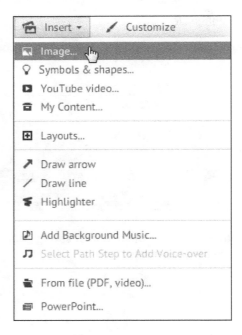

Once you have located the image (or images) that you want, these will be inserted into your prezi canvas in the same way as any other image file.

How it works...

This method ensures that the design of each slide is kept as it was originally designed in PowerPoint.

At the same time, the downside of using this method (converting to an image file format) is that you will not be able to edit any part of the material in Prezi.

See also

If you prefer to import PowerPoint slides in a way that ensures that you can edit the content of each slide as you like, refer to the next section for the third method of importing PowerPoint slides.

Reusing PowerPoint material – method 3

In this section, we will show you how to perform an import using Prezi's own import feature. This method of importing has its benefits but also a couple of drawbacks.

The really useful feature for this method of importing is that everything in your PowerPoint can be edited after the import. However, the downside is that after the import, everything will in fact need to be edited.

Be aware that when you use this feature to import content from PowerPoint, the PowerPoint design template does not get transferred. You will be transferring the content alone.

The **Insert** menu options are shown in the following screenshot:

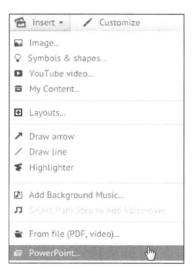

Getting ready

1. Open your prezi.

2. Zoom into an empty area of the canvas (as you may need to edit your imported PowerPoint material before before deciding the final placements for it).

How to do it...

1. In the prezi, click on **Insert**.

2. Choose **PowerPoint**.

3. Locate the PowerPoint file in your filesystem and click on **Open**.

4. Your slides will now appear in the window pane to the right of the canvas. At the top of this window, you will see the name of the PowerPoint file.

As shown in the following screenshot, our PPT file lost all its design and formatting features in the transfer from PowerPoint to Prezi:

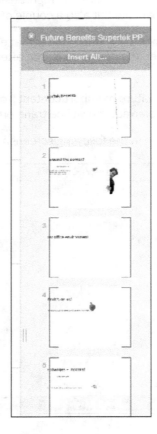

If your PowerPoint presentation contains a lot of slides or large picture files, it may be too large to import at once. If the import is aborted by the Prezi program, try dividing your file into two smaller PowerPoint files.

How it works...

Now you have the option of inserting individual slides from your PowerPoint simply by pointing to any single slide and then dragging it onto the canvas.

This is the method that we prefer for importing PowerPoint material. The reason is that this option helps us reuse only the material that works well in the Prezi media.

Your other option is to click on **Insert All** to insert all slides. **Insert All** is found at the top of the slide pane.

Both options require that you confirm your choice by clicking on the green check mark that will appear on the screen after either dragging a single slide onto the canvas or clicking on **Insert All...**, as shown in the following screenshot:

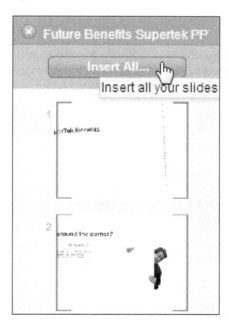

If you choose to insert all slides, then in the next step, you will be required to choose a layout. The following screenshot shows the choices available:

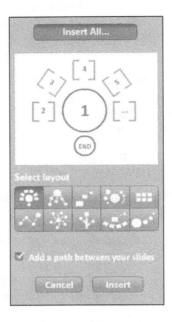

In the slides in the slide pane in the illustration on the previous page, it is easy to notice that the presentation that used to look so good (with the red lettering, bricks, and so on) has changed drastically. All the nice design features such as colors and graphics have disappeared.

What presents an even bigger challenge is that while the slides have held onto the data from the presentation, this data looks very different and out of place.

It is obvious that we will be spending some time cleaning up and reorganizing. Most text elements need to be edited for fonts, placement, and size, and we need to figure out a way to fit the content of these frames (previously known as slides) into our general design for this prezi.

All of these matters will be easier for you to sort out if the material is not organized in the fanciest layout available. For this reason, we recommend that you choose the grid layout for the frames when importing a complete PPT presentation.

In the following screenshot, the grid layout is marked with a red arrow:

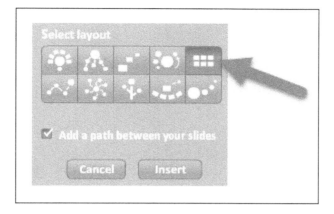

The grid layout helps you view your imported material in the best way.

See also

See guidelines for creating a beautiful and useful Prezi design in *Appendix A, Design*.

15
Sharing and Collaborating

In this chapter, we will cover the following recipes:

- ▶ Portable prezi
- ▶ The `pez` file
- ▶ Collaborating real time in Prezi
- ▶ Embedding your prezi on a website

Introduction

In today's world team work, task groups, and collaboration are the rules more than the exception.

There are a lot of situations where we need to cooperate. One day we brainstorm for a project with a group of colleagues, the next day we develop the design of a prezi in collaboration with another colleague, and the following week we create a presentation for a sales rep, and he needs it NOW.

Fortunately, all these tasks are easily performed with Prezi's great features for sharing and collaboration.

Portable prezi

The portable prezi is a great invention because it allows you to bring, send, and show your prezi anywhere.

The computer that you want to show it on does not need to have Prezi installed on it. The quality of the Internet connection is irrelevant because you can present the prezi without being online.

Getting ready

1. Go to your Prezi account and open the prezi that you want to work with.

2. Click on **Download**, as shown in the following screenshot:

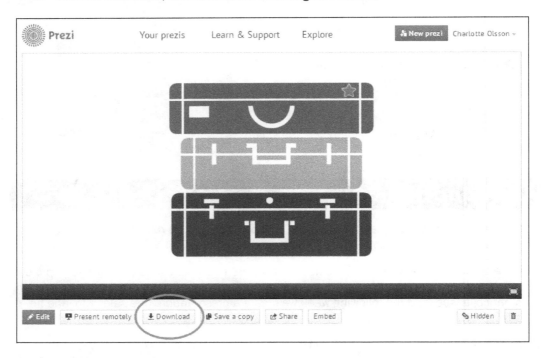

How to do it...

1. After clicking on **Download**, you have two options to download. In this section, we work with the first one, **Presenting on Windows and Mac without installation**. Take a look at the following screenshot, where the download option, marked by a blue box, will create a portable prezi:

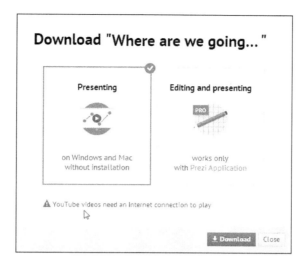

2. As soon as you hit the **Download** button, Prezi prepares to download. This will take a few minutes.

3. When the file is ready, it is delivered straight to your computer.

The portable prezi is delivered as a ZIP file. You will need to unzip the file before presenting. You may choose to unzip straight away or you can do it later.

When you unzip the folder, you will see that it has three files in it. They are called content, Prezi.app, and Prezi.exe, as shown in the following screenshot:

These three files must be together for the portable prezi to work.

It is of the utmost importance (yes, that sounds terrible, but this is really important) that you always keep these three files together. If they are not all present and together when you want to run your portable prezi, it will not work.

If you are bringing or sending a portable prezi somewhere or to someone, use the original .zip file. Unzip before the presentation. Then you'll know that everything you need for presenting is in it.

How it works...

The portable prezi can be taken anywhere and can be shown on almost any computer that you can breathe just a little life into. It does not matter whether it is a Mac or a Windows computer, and it also does not need to have Prezi installed.

You should be aware that a portable prezi cannot be edited. A portable prezi is meant for showing the presentation only. Think of it as a good thing; even in the hands of a Prezi newbie, this prezi will stay as it is, always in great shape.

There's more...

Because you are presenting offline, any videos that you want in your portable prezi should be from files that you have access to and have loaded into the prezi before you create the portable prezi.

See also

If you have Prezi for Windows/Mac installed on your computer, you can also create and use a .pez file to present offline. Read about this in the following section.

Pez – the prezi file format

For those who have Prezi for Windows/Mac installed in their computer, downloading to the pez format is offered as an option. The pez format is useful for several reasons. People save theirs prezis as .pez files to avoid storing sensitive information online, and also to be able to send an editable prezi to a colleague who also uses "Prezi for Windows/Mac". The file format also works great if you want to bring an editable presentation with you on a USB stick to edit it later on a computer that has "Prezi for Windows/Mac" installed.

Getting ready

1. Go to your prezi account and open the prezi that you want to work with.
2. Click on **Download**; please refer to the first image from the *Portable prezi* recipe.

How to do it...

1. After clicking on **Download**, you have two options to download. In this section, we work with the second one, **Editing and presenting works only with Prezi Application**. Take a look at the following screenshot:

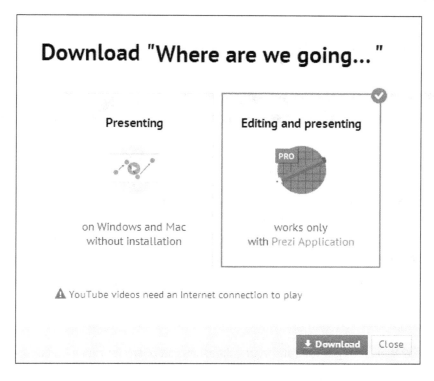

2. Right after you hit **Download**, Prezi prepares to download. This takes a few minutes.
3. When the file is ready, it is delivered straight to your computer. The file format is the .pez format.
4. Save the file to your filesystem.
5. Present your prezi offline at your convenience.

How it works...

Because you are presenting offline, any videos that you want in your pez file should be created from files that you have access to and have loaded into the prezi before creating the pez file.

There's more...

Creating pez files is an option available to subscribers of Prezi for Windows/Mac only. Likewise, the recipient of a pez file needs to have access to this program to be able to use the pez file.

It is easy to bring a `pez` file on a USB stick or send to a colleague in an e-mail. Just remember that pez files only run on computers that have Prezi for Windows/Mac.

Real-time collaboration in Prezi

Imagine that you are in your office. You sit there all by yourself (except for that third cup of coffee) while you are trying hard as can be to come up with ideas for the new spring campaign. However, it just doesn't flow.

Now Jim enters the room. After a little buddy-bantering, you show him your sketches and tell him how stuck you feel. Jim is surprised and says,

> *This here is actually a great idea. I love it! Now if you just put that line over here and move that nail/button/illustration over here to tie it all together ...*

Wouldn't it have been great if Jim had been there whole time? Well, he can be!

Prezi allows up to 20 people to access a prezi at the same time, to benefit from the synergy that comes from working together.

Sounds good? Well, let's get you (and your colleagues) on board for real-time collaboration in Prezi!

Getting ready

1. Go to the prezi that you would like to work with.
2. Click on the **Share** button as shown in the following screenshot (or inside your Prezi next to the **Exit** button):

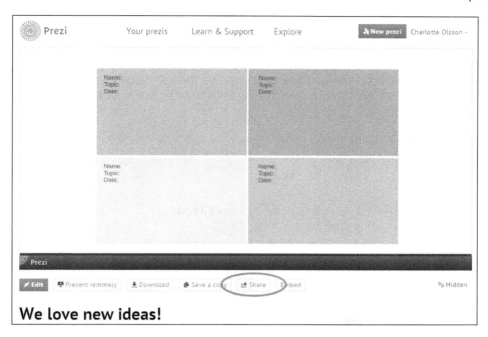

We love new ideas!

How to do it...

In the dialog box that opens after you click on **Share**, you will have to make some very important decisions. Take a look at the following screenshot and study the numbers carefully for the various sharing options:

By the number **1** (in the preceding screenshot), add the e-mail address of people you want to collaborate with in this prezi. You can invite as many as you want, and up to approximately 20 people can meet in the prezi at the same time.

By the number **2** (in the preceding screenshot), you set the setting for each individual e-mail as **Editor** or **Viewer**. A viewer can visit the prezi to see it, while an editor can visit the prezi to edit.

By the number **3** (in the preceding screenshot), is the option to copy a link to view this specific prezi. The link can then be sent in an e-mail, and provides a quick and easy way to share information.

> The e-mails that you add by the number 1 need to be connected to a prezi account to view the prezi.
>
> This is not the case for the links you create by the number 2. These links will take anybody to view the prezi.

Real-time editing in collaboration mode

Let's say you want to collaborate with your colleague, John Edwards. He is a smart guy and you'd appreciate his input in your prezi, so you add his e-mail and make him an editor.

How it works...

Later that afternoon, you and John decide to work on the prezi together. You both go to your individual computer where you log on to Prezi. You both locate the prezi and both of you click on **Edit** to go into the prezi. As soon as you are both "in", you will both be represented by an avatar, and there is a sharing panel to the right of both your screens. For this section I shared a prezi with John Edwards, as shown in the following screenshot:

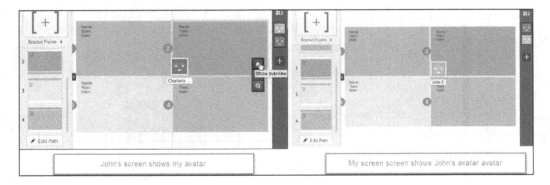

John sees my avatar on his screen, I see his on mine. John's avatar is shown on my screen on the spot that is the equivalent of the center of his screen (yep, we're hoping that this might change too). My avatar is showing on Johns' screen, letting him know the location of the centre of my current screen.

John and I can both edit all we want to. Any material that we each add to the prezi will be visible to the other party as soon as it has been entered to the canvas (textboxes have to be closed to be visible).

To the right of the screen is the collaboration panel. Click on the panel to unfold it, and you'll get access to the information and commands, as shown in the following screenshot:

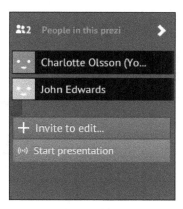

Use the collaboration panel to see who is currently in the prezi, invite more people to edit, or start a presentation.

In this panel, you can clearly see who is in the prezi and the avatar that represents them. If you think that more people need to join you, click on **+ Invite to edit** to send an e-mail to them.

Finally, anyone present in the prezi may click on the blue bar to start presenting.

Let's see how that is done.

Presenting in collaborative mode

Presenting in collaborative mode is a great way to get keep everyone oriented along the way about the progress, or at the beginning of the session, to make sure everyone is on the same page.

How it works...

John clicks on **Start presentation**. Immediately I see the following message on my screen:

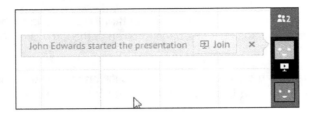

When John begins to present, I am invited to join as a viewer.

Now I have a choice to make; I can either choose to keep editing, or I can join to watch John present. I click on **Join**, and Prezi confirms. Take a look at the following screenshot:

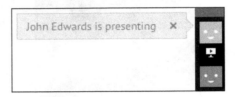

After accepting the invitation, this label confirms that I am now watching John present.

If John wants to stop presenting, or if I don't want to watch the presentation any longer, a click on the pencil icon, as shown in the following screenshot, will bring the prezi back to edit mode (yep—the same icon for both of us):

The pencil icon is used by presenters and viewers alike to go back to edit mode.

Whenever John or I think that we are done working in the prezi for now, each of us may use the **Exit** button on the top-right side of the prezi screen to exit.

The work that we did will be saved, but may of course be changed by whoever has not yet left the prezi.

Design

In this appendix, we will cover the following topics:

- ▶ The importance of design
- ▶ Basic design principles—colors, fonts, and composition
- ▶ Finding the right graphic theme

Introduction

Learning and understanding how to use Prezi's functionalities is the foundation for creating great prezis. But at some point, you may find yourself wondering what it is that constitutes the difference between a prezi that actively supports and strengthens your message, and a prezi that is just a pretty visual backdrop.

While this book is not a design manual, we would like to point you in the right direction for making conscious choices when designing your prezi. This is because design matters. Making good design choices will dramatically raise your prezi's potential to create an impact on the audience.

Maybe you have only 30 minutes to spend on designing your prezi, or maybe you have days. In any case, make design decisions that concur with your main message.

Many companies have a design manual. Ask for the manual and look into the principles for colors, fonts, and general look and feel. Typically you will find RGB color specifications, different design elements, variations of the company logo— always with examples that show you how to use these elements. Following this manual's instructions will make your prezi's design reflect the company design.

The importance of design

As a presenter, you are always the most important part of any presentation. Your clothes, body language, tone of voice, and the actual words you choose all come together to create an impact on your audience.

Your presentation's visual effects also play an important role in the experience that your audience gets when you are presenting. A prezi that is designed right supports and clarifies your communication. It makes your audience feel that they are in the hands of a professional. They will be motivated and want to hear what you have to say.

[

Create a "focus paper". Before you begin working on the canvas, spend a few minutes focusing on your message and the impression that you want to make on your audience. Write it down. As you design, reread it every now and then to help keep your creative ideas aligned with your message.
]

Consistent visual language

Visual consistency helps your audience easily understand your visual language. They will not have to spend time figuring out what your visuals mean, meaning they can spend that important time listening to you.

Be consistent by using the same set of settings (size, color, and font) for subject titles, subtitles, and body text (one set for each). Also, be consistent in your use of frames (color, size, and type).

[

A useful principle for designers of all kinds is that less is more. This applies to Prezi too! Apply the principle to colors, imagery, and overall look and feel.
]

Basic design principles – colors

Even if you are not a believer of such statements as: "red is the color of love" and "green is the color of jealousy", be aware that colors do send signals.

Make sure that the colors you use in your prezi are aligned with your message as well as with your audience. If you are not sure which colors would be a good match for your message, look for inspiration by searching the Internet for sites that work with the same topic as yours.

[

Blue, grey, and green are used often for business presentations. In such presentations, red, yellow, and orange are good choices for accent colors.
]

Important color choices

Choosing colors is a very important part of creating a good Prezi design. For some of us, it is also one of the most difficult parts of the design process. If you feel inexperienced or not naturally gifted for working with colors, consider applying our rules of thumb for your main items and your accent items respectively. Here they are:

Decide on a background color for your canvas before you choose colors for the content on the canvas. The background should be fairly neutral, which is why presenters often use white or beige. White and beige both look great in Prezi and are easy to work with. However, using a darker color for your background might also be a very good idea, as dark colors are less stressful on the eyes.

The main items are title, subtitles, and body text. Accent items are minor items, such as arrows, lines, and symbols.

Your main items look best in colors that match. Colors that match easily are colors that are related, which means that they are close to each other on the color wheel. For that reason, a great way to choose your main colors is to pick two or three colors that are related on the color wheel, shown in the following screenshot, and apply these to your main items:

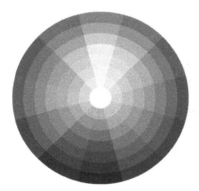

Your accent items are meant to stand out. This is easily done by picking a color from the opposite side of the color wheel for the accents (in other words, a contrasting color). If you need more than one accent color, consider choosing accent colors that are related to each other and complementary. If you choose yellow as your main color, choose accents from colors opposite to yellow.

Take a look at the following color wheel:

Color match palette

If you don't want to worry about the color wheel and related and unrelated colors, Prezi includes a tool that is very helpful. This is the color palette, as shown in the following:

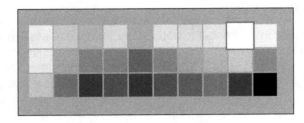

This palette helps you choose colors that look well together. Notice how each column of three colors belongs to the same section of the color wheel. Using colors from one column is an easy way to ensure that your colors match.

A great way to use this tool is to use colors from one column for your main items. This ensures that your main items will match in color.

Then pick another column for your accents from the other side of the color chart. Now your accents will match each other, while at the same time, they will stand out from the main items.

The color palette is accessed via the text toolbar (an open text box) or in the **Wizard** dialog box (by navigating to **Custom | Customize panel | Advanced**), as shown in the following screenshot:

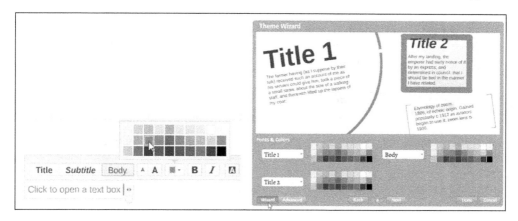

 The color choices in this palette are identical no matter which template or theme you have chosen for your prezi.

The principles applied

Now take a look at the following screenshot, where colors from the green column are used for text; orange has been chosen for highlights:

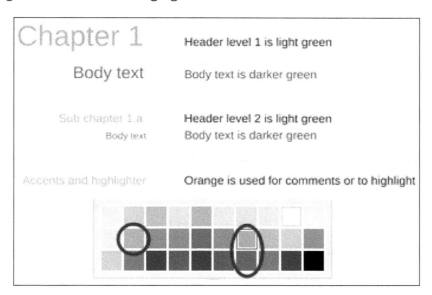

[Prezi has a collection of great color themes that are beautifully designed and ready to be applied. You can read about these in *Chapter 11, Templates, Colors, and Fonts.*]

Basic design principles – fonts

For most of us, text simply conveys content. Typically, we don't think about the design of the letters we are looking at, but even the font on your opening screen for your prezi sends a subconscious message to your audience. They will perceive this message in just a few seconds. Take a look at the fonts in the following image and see for yourself:

This is a creative presentation

This is a business presentation

Your choice of fonts set the scene for your presentation.

You need to plan for this so that your text will work for you and support your message. You do this by carefully choosing a font that matches your content and design.

No matter which set of fonts you end up choosing, make sure the body text is easy to read, and don't write too much. It is best to stick to short titles and subtitles, and small amounts of body text.

[Don't talk while your audience is reading your text (or other visuals) because they won't hear you. Whenever something changes on the Prezi screen, you should be silent for a few seconds. After the audience has understood the visuals, that's when you talk.]

Prezi's selection of fonts

Prezi comes with a great selection of fonts. You access the fonts via the **Customize** menu.

The complete selection of fonts is shown here. The selection of fonts is identical for all styles—title, subtitle, and body:

Alegreya
Aleo
Arimo
Arsenal
Cabin
БОЖЛВ ЗШЕ ФТ
From Where You Are
Heuristica
KG Empire of Dirt
KOMIKA TITLE
League Gothic
Liberation Mono Pr
Noto Sans
Playfair Display
Tinos
Titillium

Prezi offers a selection of 16 very different fonts.

The fonts in Prezi are very well-chosen. They are all beautiful, and even if the selection is currently not huge, it offers a great variety. You will be able to find fonts that suit your formal and informal presentations, and anything in between.

[

The best text for your prezi is created when you restrict yourself to keywords and avoid regular sentences that require more reading time.
]

Variations – regular, bold, and italic

All fonts can be used in four variations—regular, bold, italic, and bold + italic.

Take a look at the following font rendered in its different variations:

Regular **Bold** *Italic* ***Bold+Italic***

Apply the effect you prefer by selecting your text, and clicking on the **B** icon for bold or **I** for italics in the textbox. Repeat to remove the effect.

The different variations of a font can be used to format a whole section, such as all the words in a title or subtitle, or they can be used to make key concepts stand out. Now, take a look at the following example:

"I think the colors on the **walls** need updating. And maybe the furniture, especially the **sofa** in the corner."

Janice, Customer

Highlighting your keywords with bold, italics, or color makes it easier for your audience to read or skim the text. This means that you cut down on their reading time. Instead of reading, your audience will be listening to you. In the following example, we combined color and bold for an even stronger effect:

"I think the colors on the **walls** need updating. And maybe the furniture, especially the **sofa** in the corner."

Janice, Customer

How to use the fonts

Choose one font for your titles, another for subtitles, and a third for body text. By doing so, you make it easy for your audience to follow the structure of your presentation.

Take a look at the following examples of Prezi fonts and suggestions for use:

Alegreya Heuristica	Printed styles with a business look. Works great as headlines
Arimo Cabin	Simple, elegant, easy to read. Works well even at a small size
Comic Zine OT KG Empire of Dirt	Hand drawn, fun, and creative styles Great in small doses such as comments
Playfair Titillium	Modern styles with a sleek and innovative cool look

If your company's design manual requires the use of a specific font for your prezi, contact Prezi Sales or a Certified Prezi Expert to get help.

Any font that you have the right to use can be inserted and used in a prezi.

Basic design principles – composition

Information and visuals that are carefully chosen, well-structured, and presented in a clear design have a very convincing effect on your audience.

Creating a visual structure that clearly represents everything that is said is the presenter's best tool to impress the audience and make it easier for the audience to follow the presenter's train of thought.

The creation of a successful prezi design begins with identifying the structure of your information. Make it clear to yourself what type or structure of information you are working with so that that you know exactly how this can be reflected visually on the canvas.

To help you understand what we mean by "structure of information," we have listed three examples of common structures or types of information processes:

▸ **Chapters and subchapters**: For material that has sections, create chapter sections on your canvas so that your visuals clearly show the sections (or chapters) and the subsections for each chapter.

▸ **Development or process**: A development is best shown with a movement that goes from the left to right, or you can use right-to-left movement to signal moving backwards (remember that some cultures use directions the other way round).

▸ **Concepts or ideas**: For a presentation that involves discussion of a lot of concepts, use a mind-map-style design, where size and proximity represents relative importance.

 Use an overview picture of your prezi's structure at the beginning of your presentation as well as at the end. The initial overview helps set the scene for your message. The closing overview will serve as a mental reference for your audience.

In the following pages, we will show you three simple design examples. Each design represents one of the structures that we just described.

Design example – chapters and subchapters

The design shown in this section is ideal for presentations whose content can be easily divided into chapters or sections. Adhering to the described principles ensures that your audience has a good overview of your presentation. This will make it easier for them to understand your message.

The following are the principles of chapter composition:

▸ The title stands out and has been placed where it is clearly visible.

▸ All other categories of elements on the screen have a uniform look, and are thus easily identified. The chapter frames are identical in shape, size, and color. The subchapters are in circles and also share a uniform look, which makes them easily identifiable.

The following design structure has clearly visible chapters and subchapters:

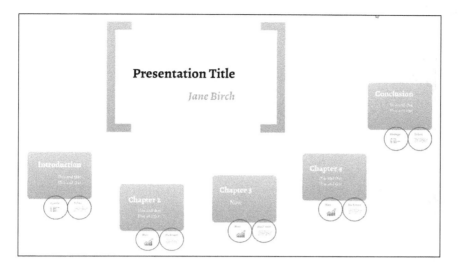

In the preceding example, we created a layout that has the title in the middle and additional material in a half circle around it. You can easily use other geometrical principles for the chapter-subchapter design that will look great.

Opening your presentation with an overview picture that shows your presentation's structure helps your audience understand where you are going. They will feel comfortable with your prezi.

Design example – development or process

A process or development is the subject for a great many presentations.

Typical examples of process presentations might be *Taking Company XYZ into the next century*, *Recipe for improving the XYZ's overhead in the next 5 years*, *Marketing for the Future*, or *Strategy and Results for Company XYZ*.

Almost any presentation about a process can be illustrated by some rendering of a forward movement. The following diagram shows a forward movement in a very simple, yet very effective and appealing way. These simple footsteps illustrate perfectly that this presentation is about a development, traveling, or a process involving change.

This design is one of the templates offered by Prezi and is a good example of the fact that design does not have to be very complicated to be useful and beautiful. Use this design, or create your own forward-moving visual to illustrate a process.

This design offers a fun side-effect: when going from one frame to the next, you will be passing over the footsteps, as shown in the following design:

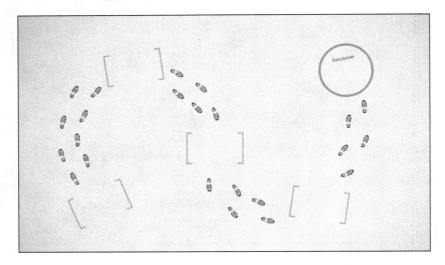

In an ideal presentation, the visuals are in sync with the content so that the visuals and the words take the audience in the same direction.

A match between your words and your visuals creates an impressing and convincing effect. For the footsteps design, such a match might be, "Let's move to the next step," or "Following the footsteps of last year's choices, let us move on."

Design example – concepts or ideas

If the purpose of your presentation is to explain related concepts or to discuss a host of ideas with your audience, using a loosely structured layout will work fine. At the same time, it will be easy for you to work with.

In a less structured layout, there is no need to arrange everything in a tight composition. Go for a free, creative style, but spend time finding a good graphic theme that will set the right "scene" for your presentation. We chose this notepad as a relevant background for taking notes at a brain-storming session.

Even if this layout is loosely or asymmetrically composed, it offers a very good overview picture if you arrange your frames so that they look nice. Take a look at the following screenshot of frames:

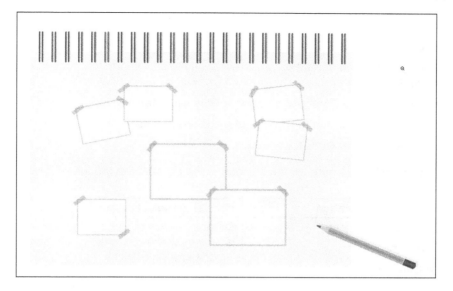

A loose layout on an informal background will also work well to show your collection of vacation photos or a series of images shown for inspiration.

 Use Prezi's **Highlighter** (by navigating to **Insert | Highlighter**) to draw a piece of "tape", or use the pins found in **Symbols** (by navigating to **Insert | Symbols & Shapes**).

Finding the right graphic theme

Finding the right graphic theme or metaphors for your presentation is the first step towards creating great visuals. Choose a graphic theme or main graphic metaphor that ties everything in your presentation together.

A theme or main metaphor will help guide your search for materials in a single direction. The purpose is to help you find graphic items that do not just work for a single item or concept in your presentation. Rather, you need to find illustrations that relate to the main concepts. This will make your presentation appear unified and focused.

Some Prezi designers sit down and work with a pen and paper during this phase. This is a great idea because you will not get distracted by playing on the prezi canvas.

Here is our recipe for searching for and developing ideas for graphic metaphors:

- ▶ Identify a main idea or overall concept that relates to your presentation as a whole.
- ▶ Identify words and metaphors you want to use to explain the information in your presentation.
- ▶ Aim for simplicity. Simplicity is easier to work with than intricacy.
- ▶ Create a list of your main ideas, words, and metaphors.
- ▶ Use this list as keywords for graphical inspiration.

Sounds complicated? No, not really. Take a look at the examples in the following table:

Words in your presentation	Idea for graphical theme
"Rise above the situation" "Reach a higher level" "Creating an overview"	Sky and aviation theme. Background of clouds or sunny skies. Aviation theme for individual illustrations. Blue colors.
"Tactics" "Strategy" "Planning and organizing"	Chess theme in black and white colors. Chessmen for individual illustrations. Checkered chess-board as background
"Organic" "Grow and bloom"	Green theme as in apples or branches. Green and red colors. Background of a tree or a field.

See also

Do you want to reuse material from your favorite PowerPoint presentations? Refer to *Chapter 14, PowerPoint and Prezi.*

B

Transitions

In this appendix, we will cover the following topics:

- ▶ Designing your transitions—Distance, Size, Turning
- ▶ Smooth transitions

Introduction

In Prezi, we use the concept of transition. This concept is used to describe the transitioning or moving forward of one frame to the next in present mode.

By carefully working with the various relationships between the frames on the Prezi canvas, we can make our presentation move forward in present mode (from one frame to the next) in a way that looks nice and supports our message.

All transitions are defined by what happens in a move from one frame to the next. Are these two frames close or far? Are they of equal or different sizes? Are they right-way-up or turned?

 Because transitions are defined by the frames on the path in your prezi, it is a good idea to work with transitions as an integrated part of the design phase.

Designing your transitions

By designing and adjusting placement, size, and turning of the frames on our canvas, we can create transitions that are nice to look at.

We can use the following three parameters to design and adjust transitions:

- ▶ Distance or proximity
- ▶ Size of the frames
- ▶ Turning of the frames

When proceeding from frame A to frame B, Prezi transitions over a distance (long or short) to a frame B that has a size (bigger, smaller, or equal compared to frame A), and could be turned or not turned (again compared to frame A).

Transitions are adjusted using the following three parameters shown in the screenshot:

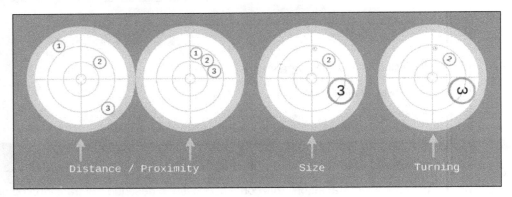

In the following sections, we'll examine each of these factors to better understand how they work.

 Any frame that has been added to the path always fills the entire screen in present mode and is shown in its right-way-up position.

Distance

Moving over big distances creates big jumps. Think of it in this way: much like an airplane, you will have to go up, then fly over the canvas, and then go down. That is a big move, and it will feel a bit like jumping.

Moving over small distances creates small moves. Think of it in this way: much like walking on a sidewalk, you move step-by-step. This is a calm move that you should use for the majority of your presentation. It is pleasant to watch and will not take away focus from your message.

Now, take a look at the following illustration of distance between the frames that impacts the viewing experience:

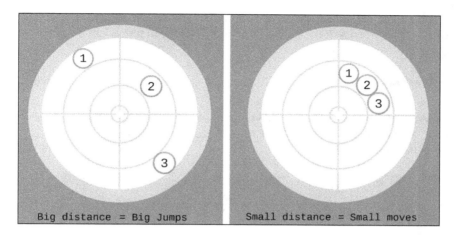

The big moves or jumps are a good choice when you want to signal that something new or different is coming up. Just be aware that if there are a lot of big jumps in your prezi, it will be unpleasant to watch.

The small moves look calm. Calm moves are a good choice for signaling that you are staying within your current topic or aspect of your presentation.

Size

In the following illustration, you will notice that the frames do not have the same size. This will add a zoom effect, because Prezi has to zoom in or out to show the frame that is next in the order of the presentation:

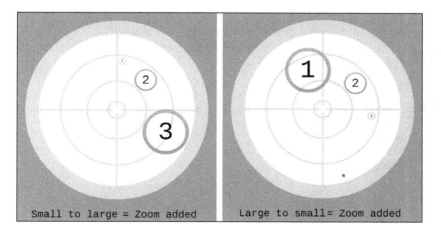

The distance between the frames impacts how jumpy the transition will feel.

The greater the difference in size, the greater the zoom effect will be. Think of it in this way: in front of a building, you will move closer to study the front door. You may then make a small move to zoom in on a detail on the door knob. But if you then want an overview of the building, you need to take a big step back.

Turning

In the following diagram, some frames have been turned. When we proceed in the presentation to show this frame, Prezi will turn the canvas so that every frame is shown the right-way-up:

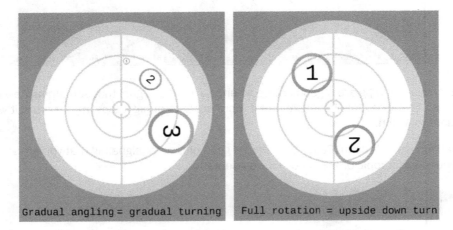

Gradual angling = gradual turning | Full rotation = upside down turn

In the image to the left shown in the preceding diagram, the viewer will experience a smooth, gradual turn, and it will be pleasant to watch. This is a good layout for content that describes aspects of the same main topic.

In the image to the right shown in the preceding diagram, Prezi will do a full upside-down turn of 180 degrees. This type of turn is impressive when used sparingly. 180-degree turns work well for opening or closing effects.

[Don't ever use turning or big jumps just because you can. Meaningless motion confuses and disengages your audience.]

See also

If you need to refresh what you learned about path and frames, you may want to read *Chapter 5, Path and Steps*, and *Chapter 6, Frames and Prezi Ratio*.

Smooth transitions

A good prezi is a prezi that does not take the focus away from you or your words, but helps you by supporting your message. A lot of flying around on the canvas, or going up and down and turning for no reason will not support your message.

The bulk of your prezi usually benefits from moving forward in harmonic steps. A very easy way to obtain harmony and a smooth flow in your presentation is to create identical frames with a short distance between them.

Placing your frames in a vertical, horizontal, or diagonal layout is an easy way to obtain harmonic, smooth transitions that are pleasant to look at.

For the smoothest move, use frames of identical size. For a smooth move in or out, use frames that change size gradually.

 A prezi's transitions cannot be adjusted to go slower, faster, or more or less jumpy.

Smooth moves with no zooming

Moving between identical frames that are placed closely or directly over or under each other, or moving between frames going to either the right or the left as a row, are easy ways of creating a nice, quiet transition without any zooming:

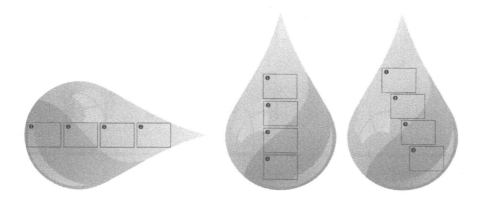

Minimal movement between identical frames creates nice, smooth moves.

The closer the frames are placed to each other, the less the jumping notion the viewer will experience when the prezi moves forward in **Present** mode.

The easiest way to create identical frames is by copying. Begin by creating the frame just the way you want it to look. Then press *Ctrl + D* to create duplicates.

Notice that copied frames are not automatically added to the path. You will have to do that yourself in the **Edit Path** mode.

Smooth moves with zooming

Sometime you will want to zoom in on a detail or zoom out to see a bigger section of the canvas, but you will want to do it in a calm, professional-looking manner.

If this is the case, anchoring is for you! A nice, calm motion is created when you "anchor" your frames to an area on the canvas.

In the following screenshot, frames 1 and 2 are placed such that their left and top corners are in the same spot. So, when we switch to present mode and go from frame 1 to frame 2, the motion will resemble taking a single step back from a picture—nice and smooth!

The "anchoring" effect provides a nice, calm motion for the transition.

Smooth move with turning

Gradual rotation can be created by turning same-sized frames gradually around a center point.

In the following diagram, we've used this principle to create a cogwheel-like motion that looks very nice when presenting:

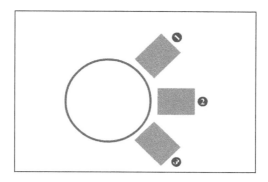

In the preceding diagram, moving from frame 1 to frame 2 and then to frame 3 creates the notion of a moving cogwheel.

The cogwheel layout is very useful for illustrating time that passes, steps in a process, or something motoric that moves forward.

[Hold down *Shift* while you turn each shape in steady 15-degree increments. This makes it easy to create gradual turns.]

Combine anchoring and turning

An easy method for creating a beautiful, smooth zooming movement is to place frames as shown in the following diagram. These frames follow an imaginary line and combine with a gentle adjustment of their sizes:

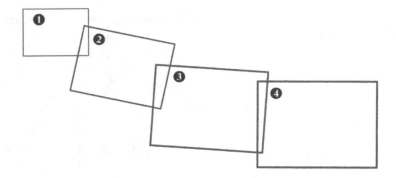

In this pattern, the frames gently go from small to large. The movement works equally well when going from large to small.

There's more...

Check your prezi for crisscross—always.

Numerous movements that make the viewer feel as if they are flying and jumping over the canvas are unnecessary, unpleasant, and distracting. Repeated use of such effects are likely to have a negative effect on the message that you are trying to convey:

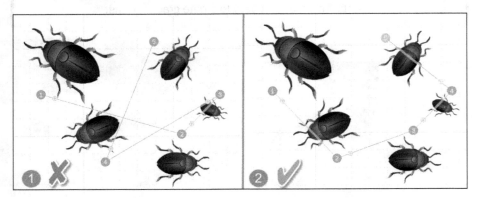

Switch to edit mode to check your path for crisscross; path 1 is a seasickness-promoting path, while path 2 is an ideal path.

Keyboard Shortcuts

Keyboard shortcuts for presenting

Keys	Action
Arrow: Right, Left	This key is used to move forward and backward along the path.
Arrow: Up, Down	This key is used to zoom in/out.
B	This key is used to blackout the screen (move your mouse or press any key to go back to presenting).
PageUp/PageDown	This key is used to move forward/backward along the path (not in full screen).
Esc	This key is used to end presentation mode.

Keyboard shortcuts for editing

Keys	Action
F	This key is used to draw frame, press again to change frame type (bracket, circle, rectangle, or hidden).
L	This key is used to load a file on your canvas (image, PDF, video).
S	This key is used to draw a shape, press again to change shape type (arrow, line, rectangle, circle, or triangle).
P	This key is used to go to **Path** mode.
1	This key is used to zoom in.
2	This key is used to zoom out.
3	This key is used to rotate clockwise.
4	This key is used to rotate counter clockwise.

Keys	Action
Delete, Backspace	This key is used to delete selected object(s).
Arrows: Left, Right, Up, Down	This key is used to move the selection 1 pixel.
Shift + Left, Right, Up, Down	This key is used to move the selection 10 pixels.
Alt + Mouse/trackpad movement	This key is used to move, resize, or rotate a frame without altering the content of that frame.
Ctrl + S	This key is used to save prezi.
Ctrl + Z	This key is used to undo last action.
Ctrl + Y	This key is used to redo last action.
Ctrl + D	This key is used to duplicate selected object(s).
Ctrl + C	This key is used to copy selected object(s).
Ctrl + V	This key is used to paste copied object(s).
Ctrl + Shift + M	This key is used to toggle screen ratio between values: 4:3, 16:9, and off.
Ctrl + Shift + C	This key is used to open the CSS editor.
Ctrl + Shift + D	This key is used to duplicate and flip your content, creating a mirrored version of your content (works for images and arrows, not for text).
Esc (Escape key)	This key is used to finish current action or close open dialog.
Spacebar	This key is used to enter the **Present** mode.

Prezi's official keyboard shortcut list is provided in the following link:

`www.prezi.com/support/article/creating/keyboard-shortcuts`

Index

About Packt Publishing

Packt, pronounced 'packed', published its first book, *Mastering phpMyAdmin for Effective MySQL Management*, in April 2004, and subsequently continued to specialize in publishing highly focused books on specific technologies and solutions.

Our books and publications share the experiences of your fellow IT professionals in adapting and customizing today's systems, applications, and frameworks. Our solution-based books give you the knowledge and power to customize the software and technologies you're using to get the job done. Packt books are more specific and less general than the IT books you have seen in the past. Our unique business model allows us to bring you more focused information, giving you more of what you need to know, and less of what you don't.

Packt is a modern yet unique publishing company that focuses on producing quality, cutting-edge books for communities of developers, administrators, and newbies alike. For more information, please visit our website at www.packtpub.com.

Writing for Packt

We welcome all inquiries from people who are interested in authoring. Book proposals should be sent to author@packtpub.com. If your book idea is still at an early stage and you would like to discuss it first before writing a formal book proposal, then please contact us; one of our commissioning editors will get in touch with you.

We're not just looking for published authors; if you have strong technical skills but no writing experience, our experienced editors can help you develop a writing career, or simply get some additional reward for your expertise.

Instant Prezi Starter

ISBN: 978-1-84969-702-6   Paperback: 56 pages

A user-friendly, step-by-step introductory guide to using Prezi, a web-based presentation application program ideal for engaging your audience

1. Learn something new in an Instant! A short, fast, focused guide delivering immediate results.

2. Amaze your audience and keep them engaged during your presentations with Prezi.

3. Learn with the help of practical resources for awesome examples and inspiration.

Prezi HOTSHOT

ISBN: 978-1-84969-977-8   Paperback: 264 pages

Create amazing Prezi presentations through 10 exciting Prezi projects

1. Amaze your audience and keep them engaged during your presentations with Prezi.

2. Create interactive presentations from scratch by adding images, animations, and more.

3. Learn Prezi through ten exciting projects in this step-by-step tutorial.

Please check **www.PacktPub.com** for information on our titles

Building Impressive Presentations with impress.js

ISBN: 978-1-84969-648-7   Paperback: 124 pages

Design stunning presentations with dynamic visuals and 3D transitions that will captivate your colleagues

1. Create presentations inside the infinite canvas of modern web browsers.

2. Build presentations that work anywhere, any time, and on any device.

3. Build dynamic presentations with rotation, scaling, transforms, and 3D effects.

Instant HTML5 Presentations How-to

ISBN: 978-1-78216-478-4   Paperback: 64 pages

Create beautiful and functional presentations using the reveal.js library, HTML5, and CSS3

1. Learn something new in an Instant! A short, fast, focused guide delivering immediate results.

2. Create presentations using HTML5 and run them straight from your browser.

3. Easily publish presentations on your website by using modern web technologies.

Please check **www.PacktPub.com** for information on our titles